Bolly

Popular Indian Cinema

wood

Edited by Lalit Mohan Joshi

FOREWORD

Derek Malcolm

Mention the word Bollywood to those who have only the vaguest ideas about Indian films and they will probably say: 'Oh yes – songs and dances, wet saris and romantic melodrama for the semi-literate masses'. The only Indian filmmaker of whom they have heard is probably Satyajit Ray, who doesn't do that sort of thing at all.

They would, of course, be half right. Bollywood, or the mostly Hindi films emanating from Mumbai, has produced some of the most feeble and repetitive films in the world. But then, so has Hollywood. It is more than time to admit that Bollywood, just like Hollywood, is capable of good things as well and has played host to a whole string of directors, musicians, singers and actors who can legitimately be called artists of the first order. Even the word Bollywood implies, to many who work out of Bombay, a kind of patronizing put-down which is made worse by the fact that filmmakers from the whole of South India are often lumped together under the same title.

This book, aimed as much at those ignorant of Indian cinema as at those familiar with it in its popular form, attempts to prove that whether you like the term Bollywood or regret it, there is real quality involved as well as quantity. As a western critic with The Guardian, I welcome it wholeheartedly. It is not a fan's hagiography, valuable only to those who adore Bollywood. Nor is it a worthy academic tome through which to wade yawning. It tries instead to understand Bollywood, warts and all, and to explain its huge appeal through the last several decades of its history. It looks at India and Indians as well as the films and it gives us the clues we need to understand Bollywood better.

My own view is that Bollywood in general is just beginning to climb back out of the artistic trough into which it sank after its great days in the forties and fifties, and that now is the time to pay attention to it again not merely as an Indian phenomenon but as a significant part of world cinema.

I recently had the doubtful pleasure, as a mere westerner, of trying to explain Bollywood to a group of media students from Harvard and Yale. It was a difficult task, and I wish I'd had this book beside me at the time. But even without it, and often with unsubtitled excerpts from famous Bollywood films like *Mother India*, *Pyaasa* and *Pakeezah*, the students were captivated and wanted to learn more.

What they saw was often unabashed melodrama, but it was stories told by real film-makers, aided by stars, musicians and playback singers who often had every right to be compared with the best of those from Hollywood. The films seemed to capture their imaginations, perhaps because of, rather than in spite of, their alien culture. But they genuinely appreciated the art, craftsmanship and conviction that went into their making.

I have to admit that, as a critic, an unrelieved diet of Bollywood would send me as insane as the constant diet of Hollywood I have often had to endure. But when I sometimes shuffle in my seat at a routine Bollywood epic, I try to remember the many occasions when I have been surprised and delighted by them. And I often recall the moment at the BBC when a young World Service producer asked me whether, on the sad announcement of Raj Kapoor's death, his programme ought to carry an obituary.

Not knowing much about Raj, he seemed doubtful. Just then, I noticed an Indian woman outside the studio at Bush House. So I went outside and told her, in front of the producer, that Raj Kapoor had died. She immediately broke into tears. We did the obituary. Satyajit Ray, I said, had made films about the people. Raj made films for the people. And that, now I come to think of it, is what Bollywood is all about.

Bollywood 100 Years

Cinema in India has evolved as a parallel culture. Although it came from the West, it derived strength from a whole range of Indian myths, legends, folk and theatrical forms. As an art form, it was internalized. Indian film today has come a long way and reflects a distinct ethos. Its uniqueness lies in its form, its manner of telling a story, its way of building up tensions in the narrative and the fashion in which they are released.

In *Lagaan* (2001), for example, the film-maker Ashutosh Gowarikar uses anti-British sentiment as the chief ingredient to create conflict, and builds up a thrilling climax through a cricket match. Although the film has a simple narrative, its rural milieu, taut script and stunning sound effects keep the viewer absorbed. In some ways, Shyam Benegal's latest film *Zubeidaa (*2001*),* with a star cast, a powerful script and a good sprinkling of songs composed by A. R. Rahman, marks the turning of a pioneer of Indian 'new wave' cinema towards the traditional format of filmmaking. A passionate period film, it has done remarkably well in the overseas market.

'Bollywood' – Hindi Cinema with Global Appeal

'Bollywood' stands for popular Hindi films possessing mass appeal. The popularity of Indian cinema first broke national barriers in the 1950s when Raj Kapoor and Nargis, through films such as *Awara* (1951) and *Shree 420* (1955), became pin-ups in the erstwhile USSR and the Middle East. The term 'Bollywood' has gained currency during the last decade, owing to its frequent use by the western media. Although many film artistes and critics of Indian origin consider it a product of negative stereotyping, the term has also been popularized by the mushroom growth of Indian cable television networks all over the globe, with their heavy emphasis on Hindi cinema-based programmes and chat shows.

Right from 1896, Mumbai (formerly Bombay) has been the epicentre of this dream world. Bollywood knows no barriers – political, religious or man-made. Despite an official ban, pirated copies of new releases manage to reach Pakistan long before they are available in Mumbai. Indian cinema has always been a role model for filmmakers all over South Asia. The ultimate dream of many a Pakistani, Sri

The father of Indian
cinema, Dada Saheb
Phalke, viewing a film reel.
RAJA HARISHCHANDRA
(1913) was his first feature
film to be made in India.

Lankan or Nepali artist es a place in Mumbai, the film capital of India. Among contemporary actresses, Manisha Koirala is from Nepal and Zeba, the heroine of Raj Kapoor's *Heena* (1991), came to act in the film from Pakistan. Pakistan's legendary singer, the late Nusrat Fateh Ali Khan, sang for many Bollywood films and his voice was considered a valuable commercial ingredient.

The Beginning – Silent Era

The story of cinema in India is as fascinating and eventful as the history of the medium itself. The first moving images – described by the Lumière Brothers as 'the Marvel of the Century', 'the wonder of the world' – came to India barely six months after they had enthralled the west at a Paris café.

A *Times of India* advertisement of 7 July 1896 invited Bombay residents to Watson's Hotel to watch 'cinematographe' with 'living photographic pictures in lifesize reproductions'. The thrill and amazement of a running train and ladies and soldiers on wheels, became imprinted on the Indian psyche and opened up a whole new world of possibilities. Traditional art forms such as *Ramleela* (dramatisation of the story of Lord Rama), *Nautanki*

(a form of Indian folk entertainment) and the Parsi Theatre were sucked into the cinema and evolved into a new *avatar* (reincarnation) of mass entertainment now called Bollywood.

One of those who took instant inspiration from the cinematographe was the photographer Harishchandra Sakharam Bhatvadekar, who had a photo studio in Bombay since 1880. He was the first to dream of filmmaking in India when he ordered a motion picture camera from London at a price of 21 guineas. In 1897, Bhatvadekar photographed a wrestling match at Bombay's Hanging Gardens and the film was sent to London for processing. In 1901 he made India's first indigenous documentary, about an Indian student, R.P. Paranjpye, who had won distinction in mathematics at Cambridge. He is also remembered for filming the coronation of Edward VIII in 1903.

The rapid pace of events made newly arrived motion pictures commercially viable. Cinema entered Calcutta (now Kolkata), then the capital of British India. Fascinated by the new medium, Jamsetji Framji Madan, a wealthy member of the entrepreneurial Parsi community, ordered cinema projectors from Pathé and set up 'bioscope' tents at several

spots in the city. By 1910 cinema halls had
sprung up in all major Indian cities and
touring bioscopes had reached several
small towns.

Phalke – Making a Start

Cinema had arrived, but it was yet to develop
a native form. To succeed, it required mass
appeal. It was Dhundiraj Govind Phalke who
realized this by default. Phalke hailed from a
priestly family based in Trimbakeshwar (near
Nasik) and was the son of a Sanskrit scholar,
Daji Shastri. At forty, he was looking for a new
profession after the failure of a printing

venture. It was during Christmas, while
watching a film called *Life of Christ,* that the
latent potential of cinema struck him. He
imagined a surging crowd of Indians. What if
Christ was replaced by Lord Krishna? For
Phalke, it was the end of his drift.

Fired with zeal, Phalke mortgaged his life
insurance policy and raised enough money to
visit London to buy film equipment. After two
weeks of shopping, he returned to India with a
Williamson camera, a perforating machine,
developing and printing equipment, some raw
film stock and unbounded determination and
will-power.

SHIRAZ

Enakshi Ramarao and
Charu Roy starred in this
historical romance set in
the Mughal Empire. It was
directed by Franz Osten
who was employed by
Himansu Rai for many of
Bombay Talkies films.

His debut film, *Raja Harishchandra* (1913), was the story of a legendary king of ancient India whose life exemplified the pursuit of the ideal of truth. It triggered the trend of mythologicals that was to dominate the silent era. For Phalke, the film was a labour of love. He had to fight social prejudice. Acting was considered to be beyond the pale. Unable to find female actresses, he had to console himself with a delicate-looking male called Salunke, playing the role of Harishchandra's wife, Taramati. Despite hurdles, Phalke was the uncrowned king of the silent era, completing twenty mythologicals and ninety short films. His later film, *Shri Krishna Janma* (1918), has a distinct message of tolerance in its last sequence, where people from all castes offer obeisance to Lord Krishna.

Besides mythologicals, the silent era also drew inspiration from contemporary social reality. Prominent filmmakers who explored social issues were Chandulal Shah, Baburao Painter and Dhirendra Ganguly. Chandulal Shah's *Gun Sundari* (1927) depicts a husband-wife relationship in the context of a changing urban society. Baburao Painter's *Savkari Pash* (1925) documents the exploitation of the rural poor by grabbing moneylenders and contains the germs of early realistic cinema. Dhiren Ganguly's comedy *England Returned* (1921) mocks at Indians who go to the West and return with ideas that make them misfits in their own land.

The earthiness and grandeur of silent cinema lay in its being just the opposite of what the word silent connotes. It was a loud

event where people enjoyed the screen contents to the accompaniment of live sound effects created by the harmonium as well as percussion instruments such as the *tabla* and *dholak*. Far from being mute observers, audiences participated by joining the chorus of clapping and thumping.

This initial phase of cinema laid the groundwork for what was to follow. Many filmmakers including Debaki Bose, P. C. Barua, Shantaram and Mehboob, who began their innings in this period, became legends of the Sound Era. But Phalke, who had prepared the base for the growth of a prolific film industry, grew increasingly out of touch. 'Sound', a boon for cinema, dealt him a hard blow. It turned the spotlight away from him. Nevertheless, Phalke was aware of the value of his achievements. 'If I had not had the courage and daring, the film industry would never have been established in India in 1912', he remarked a short time before he died in abject poverty. The institution of the Dada Saheb Phalke Award by the government of India in 1969, his birth centenary year, indicates the truth of Phalke's claims, as does the burning desire of every Indian filmmaker to win this highly coveted award.

Censorship

The 1920s were a period when the movement for freedom from British colonial rule gathered momentum under Gandhi and other leaders. The government grew paranoid about films being used as tools to stir up patriotism and anti-British sentiment. While the censors let amorous kissing scenes and exposed body parts sail past, their eagle eyes did not miss any shot with even the faintest potential to create trouble for the ruling power. They were unperturbed by Devika Rani in *Karma* (1933), passionately kissing Himanshu Rai in a lying position. On the other hand, they banned films like *Bhakta Vidur* (1921) and *Vande Mataram Ashram* (1927), the former because it showed Vidur dressed up as Gandhi, and the latter because it criticized the educational policy of the British in India.

Sound Era – Alam Ara

A sense of unease filled the air by the late 1920s. The world's first talkie, *Jazz Singer* had been premiered in New York in 1927. Desperation marked Indian producers when a sound feature, *Melody of Love,* was shown in India in 1929. The writing was on the wall – if films did not change, they were doomed.

Filmmaker V. Shantaram.
In 100 years of Bollywood
history, Shantaram's film
making dominated for more
than 60 years.

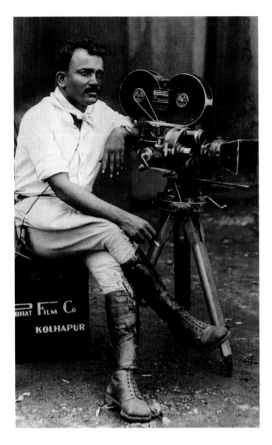

opposite page
Nadia, aka Fearless Nadia
due to her stunt acts in many
Indian films. She was born in
Australia and worked in the
Russian circus before moving
into film.

Sheikh Fatehlal, one of the
early pioneers of the silent
era. When Shantaram set
up Prabhat Studios,
Fatehlal became a partner
and went on to direct
several talkies including
SANT TUKARAM.

Ardeshir Irani recording
ALAM ARA. With basic
techniques, equipment
and studios, it was difficult
to record the first talkies;
Irani employed a sound
technician from Hollywood
for this film.

It was inevitable.

Ardeshir Irani wanted to leave nothing to
chance. Born in 1885, he had started off in the
family business of musical instruments and
later moved into foreign film distribution.
Now he craved a place in history. Having
seen Hollywood's forty per cent sound film
Showboat, he was determined to direct a
hundred per cent talkie. A rival company vying
for this honour was Madan Pictures of Calcutta
which was producing a comedy, *Jamai Sashti*
(1931). Irani snatched the laurels by a month.
When *Alam Ara* was released on 14 March
1931, Bombay's Majestic Theatre was
besieged. Tickets disappeared into the black
market while police struggled to control
people's frenzy to witness this history being
made on the screen.

Produced by the Imperial Film Company,
Alam Ara was based on a popular stage play
and starred Zubeida, Master Vithal, Prithviraj
Kapoor and W. M. Khan. Its ten songs made an
astonishing impact. Unfortunately, not even a
fragment of this historical film is preserved for
posterity. The desperate circumstances of its
making prevented it from being an artistic
triumph. 'There were no sound proof studios…
we preferred to shoot indoors … Our studio

was located near a railway track, trains
would pass every few minutes so most of
our shooting was done when trains ceased
operations. We worked with single system
Tanar recording equipment, unlike today's
double system which allows for separate
negatives for picture and sound…
Microphones had to be hidden in incredible
places to keep them out of camera range',
Irani recalled in an interview.

1930s – Rise of Studios

Sound brought immense possibilities. Cinema
now started attracting a broad cross-section
of society. Among them: the artiste, for fame
and glory; the writer for creative satisfaction,
the business class, for making a fortune; and
the masses, for joy. Film companies proliferated in Bengal, Maharashtra and South India,
but the three studios who contributed most
to an early flowering of great films were New
Theatres (Calcutta), Prabhat (Pune, now Film
and Television Institute of India) and Bombay
Talkies. It was on their solid foundations that
the grand edifice of the 'Golden 1950s' was
to rest.

New Theatres were founded in 1931 by B.
N. Sircar. A qualified engineer from London,

Sircar was drawn into film production by a sense of vision. He wanted cinema to reflect society and literature. But the medium of cinema was raw. Sound had just been introduced, as a basic function. No one had a clue how to tap sound creatively. One of the first to do so was Debaki Bose who joined New Theatres at its inception. Bose's first sound film was *Chandidas* (1932) in Bengali, which he remade in Hindi as *Puran Bhagat* (The Devotee, 1933). *Puran Bhagat* is the story of a sixteenth-century Vaishnava poet-saint. Bose's use of sound and music made it a landmark film. Both legend and history were the sources of his themes. His next film, *Vidyapati* (1937), also created a new perception of music in cinema. According to the well-known musicologist, Vanraj Bhatia, '[It] altered the conception of quality and function of music in a film'. Another luminary of New Theatres was P. C. Barua, who directed *Devdas* (1935). The film gave a break to an unknown salesman, Kundan Lal Saigal, and paved the way for his stardom both as an actor and a singer. Kidar Sharma who wrote the dialogues and lyrics of the film and Bimal Roy, its cameraman, waited for their turn to become celebrities. New Theatres became a launch pad for many

others. Works of Debaki Bose and P. C. Barua gave the studios a touch of class and elitism. Generally, it was believed that cinema halls showing their films had empty front seats and packed balconies.

V. Shantaram set up Prabhat Film Company in Kolhapur in 1929 along with four other partners – V.G. Damle, K.R. Dhaiber, S.B. Kulkarni and S. Fatehlal. Free of any elitist pretensions, they all belonged to the educated lower middle class and wanted to make socially relevant films with mass appeal. The company moved to Pune in 1933. Although early Prabhat films were in Marathi, their content had an all-India appeal.

Prabhat's *Duniya Na Mane* (1937), is even now, one of the most representative films on the rights of women in a tradition-bound society. Young Nirmala resists with determination her marriage to a man her father's age. Similarly, Shantaram's *Admi* (1939) challenged some social traditions.

Founded by Himansu Rai and his wife Devika Rani in 1934, Bombay Talkies was another institution that created an enduring film culture in India. The couple had achieved celebrity status during their stay in Europe. Rai had carved a niche for himself through

international co-productions that resulted in the making of four films – *The Light of Asia* (1926), *A Throw of Dice* (1930), *Shiraz* (1928) and *Karma (1933)*.

Based on the life of Buddha (played by Himansu Rai), *The Light of Asia* was directed by German filmmaker, Franz Osten. It proved a roaring success in Europe but failed to impress Indian viewers. *A Throw of Dice* was inspired by the *Mahabharata* tale where the Pandavas lost their kingdom in a gambling session. Set in the Mughal period, *Shiraz* depicted the legendary love-story that led to the building of the Taj Mahal. *Karma,* starring Devika Rani and Himanshu Rai, was premiered in London. Shot and synchronized at Stoll Studios in London, it was made for audiences in the West. Although Devika Rani was highly acclaimed by the British press for her perform-ance and her chaste English, the film had a very naïve plot and bombed badly. It may have acted as an eye-opener, for after *Karma*, the couple concentrated on settling in India and became committed to a cinema that was relevant to India's teeming millions.

Bombay Talkies emerged as a high-profile studio equipped with modern facilities. German technicians supervised production and trained local talent. Its early films were directed by Franz Osten. The first outstanding production was *Achchut Kanya* 1936, creating the classic conflict of a high-caste Brahmin boy falling in love with a low-caste untouch-able girl. The country was passing through its freedom struggle under the leadership of Mahatma Gandhi, who was also pioneering a movement against untouchability. This added a background of reality and helped to bring success within its reach.

On a practical level too, Bombay Talkies' intrinsic faith in equality was practically reflected in the treatment of its staff. Everyone, irrespective of caste distinctions, ate together at the company canteen. It was also not unusual for even their top actors to perform supposedly menial tasks. Four film personalities who had their initial grooming in Bombay Talkies were Ashok Kumar (who was first a lab assistant), Dilip Kumar (an actor), Raj Kapoor (a clapper boy) and Khwaja Ahmed Abbas (a scriptwriter).

This was a time when the big three vied for excellence. New Theatres even tried to involve India's Nobel Laureate Rabindranath Tagore in cinema. Tagore allowed several of his stories to be adapted for the screen. 'The principal

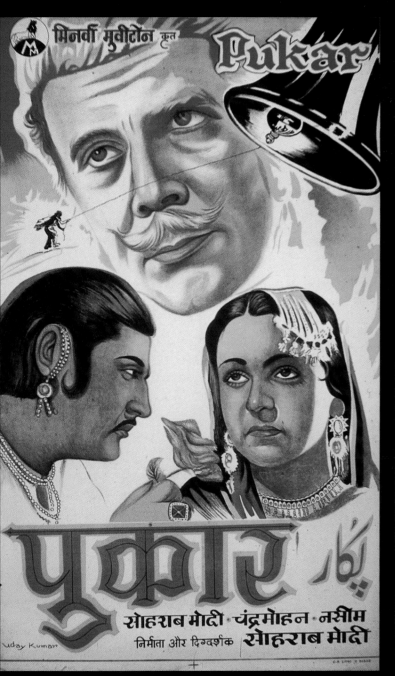

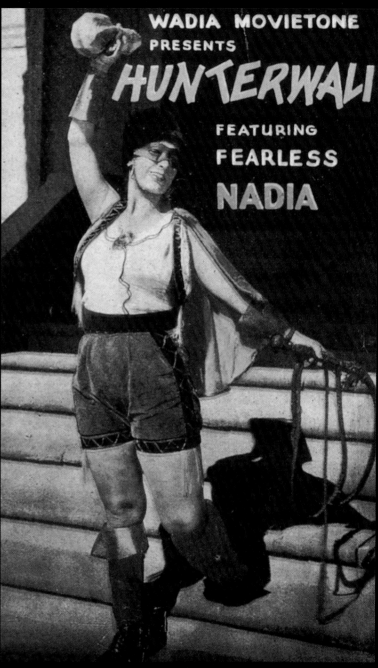

Posters have always been
the chief publicity tool of
Bollywood Cinema. The
poster on the right shows
Fearless Nadia, India's
most famous stunt actress.

element of a motion picture is the "flux of
images". The beauty and grandeur of this form
in motion has to be developed in such a way
that it becomes self-sufficient without the use
of words', he said.

Other Film Companies

Among the other impressive studios of the
1930s was Sohrab Modi's Minerva Movietone
which specialized in period films. A strong
element of popular Hindi cinema, especially of
period films, has always been dialogue. Good
films with low-key dialogues have often failed
whereas bad films with exciting dialogues
have made it at the box-office. Sohrab Modi
came from theatre. His talent for spectacle and
oratory resulted in excellent period films such
as *Pukar* (1939) and *Sikandar* (1941). He often
shot his movies in historical palaces and build-
ings to give them an authentic ambience.
Another Modi characteristic was that he
always wrote his dialogues himself.

Visually stunning films were also created
by Ranjit Film Company, Wadia Movietone and
Sagar Film Company, where Chandulal Shah,
Kidar Sharma, A.R. Kardar, Nandlal Jaswantlal
and Mehboob directed their early films.

World War – Bad News for Studios, Good News for Stars

While studios were in the midst of this
creative phase, the Second World War broke
out in 1939. British India needed guns, bombs
and ammunition for soldiers. A spurt in industrial activity created massive profits and
wealth that were translated into black money.
Profiteers jumped into the film business with
the aim of making quick gains. Film actors
began to be offered huge fees by this new
breed of producers with an added lure: part of
the fee would be in the form of black money, in
other words, tax-free. Such factors altered the
ball game. Stars became bigger than the
studios which had employed and created
them in the first place.

Filmmakers started to desert their mentors
and build up their own standing. Either they
became freelance or they established their
own company. Kidar Sharma, a legendary
lyricist and scriptwriter who had written
for *Devdas* and *Vidyapati* (1938) left New
Theatres to set up on his own. Likewise,
V. Shantaram, after directing a series of films
for Prabhat, founded Rajkamal Kala Mandir in
1943 and made several important films. By the
mid-1940s, the studio system finally gave way

Posters of **PARDESI** and
JAILOR, from the late 1930s
and early 1940s.

to a new order: from now on stars were to rule the roost.

The first star to establish his own company (RK Films) was Raj Kapoor: and the first film he made was *Aag* (1948). Around the time when Raj Kapoor and Dilip Kumar were establishing their credentials as stars, Mumbai also began to draw fresh talent from all over the country. Among the new entrants was Dev Anand, a shy young graduate from Government College Lahore. No one took him seriously at first. He seemed to lack the seasoned acting talent of Dilip Kumar or the man-of-the-street image of Raj Kapoor. Despite this, he became Indian cinema's first matinee idol with *Ziddi* (1948), and he remained at the top for more than thirty years through sheer hard work and determination.

1940s – The Brighter Side

The sense of vision, discipline and overall commitment inculcated by the early studio *gurus* did not disappear as a result of the birth of the star system. The continuing efforts of Mehboob Khan, Kidar Sharma and Bimal Roy laid the foundation for the 1950s.

Mehboob Khan founded Mehboob Productions in 1942. He chose the hammer-and-sickle as his insignia, possibly as a reminder of his own poverty-stricken past. Mehboob was a self-taught man with no formal education. He had run away from his village in Gujarat at sixteen to become an actor, and during the silent era, had worked as an extra. Mehboob's *Aurat* (1940) defined his roots and his obsession with portraying on celluloid, the pain of the rural poor. *Aurat* is also about the dignity, sacrifice and glory of motherhood. His subsequent films, *Anmol Ghadi* (1946) and *Andaz* (1949), confirmed his position as a major filmmaker of his times.

The multi-talented Kidar Sharma made significant contributions to Indian cinema as a lyricist, dialogue/script writer and a popular filmmaker. The songs he wrote for Barua's *Devdas* (1936) won celebrity status for K.L. Saigal and are still popular among South Asian music lovers. His film *Neel Kamal* (1947) also introduced two major stars of the Golden Era, Raj Kapoor and Madhubala.

Bimal Roy made his mark in the 1940s basically as a cinematographer and shot many significant films including P.C. Barua's *Devdas*. He directed his first Hindi film *Humrahi* in 1945.

PRITHVIRAJ
NARGIS
RAJ KAPOOR
IN

AWĀRA

DIRECTED
RAJ KAPOOR

The IPTA Factor

While cinema had its ups and downs as a
result of the war, other factors, such as the
struggle against British rule and the attempts
to heal the Hindu-Muslim communal divide,
had converted India into a kind of social and
political melting pot. For the cultured, earthy,
sensitive and conscientious, it provided sump-
tuous food for thought. The restlessness was
not confined to Bombay, but was an all-India
phenomenon. Nothing was tangible, but
something seemed to be happening all
around. The situation called for a revival of
India's age-old traditions of folk, drama, music
and story-telling. Attempts were made to
engineer a cultural revolution to set things
right. Out of this, in 1943, came the Indian
People's Theatre Association (IPTA). Its
founders included writers, poets, theatre
activists and film people, most notably Khwaja
Ahmed Abbas, Krishan Chander, Rajendra
Singh Bedi, Sahir Ludhianvi, Kaifi Azmi, Balraj
Sahni, Majrooh Sultanpuri, Chetan Anand and
Gulzar. They met regularly to discuss ideas
and plays. They even supported the making of
films, including Chetan Anand's debut film
Neecha Nagar (1946), an experimental film
about class conflict that received an award at

the First Cannes Festival in 1947. IPTA also
tried to uphold some of the core values of the
studio system, a true commitment to cinema
and to fine art.

The Ultimate Height of the 1950s

To call the 1950s the golden era of Indian
cinema may sound a bit trite, but this was
certainly a period when a good number of
Indian filmmakers reached the highwater
mark of their creativity. The golden era did not
appear out of the blue. It was a culmination of
all that had happened after *Raja
Harishchandra* and *Alam Ara*.

The 1950s threw up many legendary filmmakers but it was Raj Kapoor who stole the
limelight with *Awara* (1951). The film set the
agenda for popular cinema, it had all the
ingredients of a block buster – a well-written
story by the IPTA protégé Khwaja Ahmed
Abbas, lyrics by Shailendra, an earthy poet
with a leftist trade union background and
music by Shankar-Jaikishen. *Awara* broke
international barriers and gained mass popularity. Dubbed into Turkish, Persian, Arabic
and Russian, it broke box-office records in the
Middle East and drew vast crowds in the erstwhile USSR. Songs like *Echak daana, beechak*

daana were on many Russians' lips. Although
Raj Kapoor was the son of theatre celebrity
Prithviraj Kapoor, his success was not a result
of his being given any privileges. He worked
hard to move from one stage of filmmaking to
the next.

Kapoor's *Shree 420* was a variation of the
same theme as *Awara*. The title is drawn from
section 420 of the Indian Penal Code, under
which cheats and frauds are prosecuted. Raj
Kapoor's dominance of Indian cinema as a
filmmaker continued after political freedom
came to India in 1947. It extended right into
the early 1970s, when he made hit films like
Bobby (1973).

Another star to come into his own in the
1950s was the debonair Dev Anand. After Raj
Kapoor, he was the second major actor to start
an independent banner, setting up Navketan in
1949 with his brother, Chetan Anand.
Navketan exemplified the art of popular
cinema – a cinema that was entertaining but
not mindless. Its second production, *Baazi*
(1951), became a milestone for many reasons.
It was Guru Dutt's debut film as director, and it
also launched the outstanding Urdu leftist poet
Sahir Ludhianvi as lyricist, as well as music
maestro S.D. Burman as a music director.

The third major star to complete the triad
of post-independence cinema was Dilip Kumar
(original name Yusuf Khan). Dilip Kumar's
versatile image – he had more histrionic talent
than Raj Kapoor or Dev Anand – was carved by
directors such as Mehboob in *Andaz*, Kidar
Sharma in *Jogan* (1951) and Zia Sarhadi in
Footpath (1953).

Zia Sarhadi himself came into the limelight
as a filmmaker of substance with two landmark films of the early 1950s – *Humlog* (1951)
and *Footpath*. *Humlog* documents the plight of
the struggling lower middle class after independence. The film became a launch pad for
Balraj Sahni, one of the most sensitive actors

Posters of Bimal Roy's
DO BIGHA ZAMIN and
BANDINI.

of Bollywood. *Footpath* unravels the world of
black-marketeers callously hoarding medi-
cines in a famine-striken area. Before coming
to direction, Sarhadi had established his reputation as a star dialogue writer who wrote
several early scripts for Mehboob. Sarhadi's
career went into decline in the late 1950s, after
he left for Pakistan, where his talents were
muzzled under General Zia's authoritarian
regime.

The Big Three – Bimal Roy, Mehboob and Guru Dutt

It is perhaps not wrong to say that the most
remarkable feature of the decade was that it
marked the culmination of Bimal Roy's film
craft. *Do Bigha Zamin* (1953) and *Madhumati*
(1958) provide two instances of his excellence.
Nearly fifty years after it was made, *Do Bigha
Zamin* continues to mirror the exploitation of
the rural poor. *Madhumati* is entertaining as
well as artistically rich.

Roy's blending of the elements of neo-
realism and popular cinema was exceptional.
Devdas (1955), *Sujata (*1959) and *Bandini*
(1963) all reflect his deep social concerns.
Supremely versatile, he would have been
equally suited to so-called art house *avant-*

garde cinema club films of the likes of Ray or
Mrinal Sen, or the commercially viable genre of
Raj Kapoor. Bimal Roy, however, followed his
own instincts. His filmmaking shunned
artistic pretence and showed an equal disregard for glamour and fortune-hunting. His
straightforward approach won him millions of
viewers. Roy created the tragic hero mantle for
Dilip Kumar in *Devdas*. Through films such as
Sujata and *Bandini,* he gave Nutan an everlasting artistic dignity. He was also responsible for the flowering of music directors like
S. D. Burman and Salil Chowdhury. Among his
most creative pupils are filmmaker Hrishikesh
Mukherjee and lyricist/filmmaker Gulzar.

As for Mehboob, his *Mother India* (1957)
turned him into an icon. A remake of his earlier
Aurat, the film is centred around the adversi-
ties of a poor but dignified village woman. The
film underlines the conflict of values in post-
independent India. Though Mehboob's contribution to popular cinema is immense, *Mother
India* overshadows the rest of his work.

Along with *Mother India,* another big
success of 1957 was Guru Dutt's *Pyaasa*,
which unravels the tragic turn of events in a
poet's life. The strength of Guru Dutt's cinema
work lay in his ability to employ song and

Poster of **MOTHER INDIA**, Mehboob's all time favourite; the first Bollywood production to win an Oscar nomination in the Best Foeign Film category.

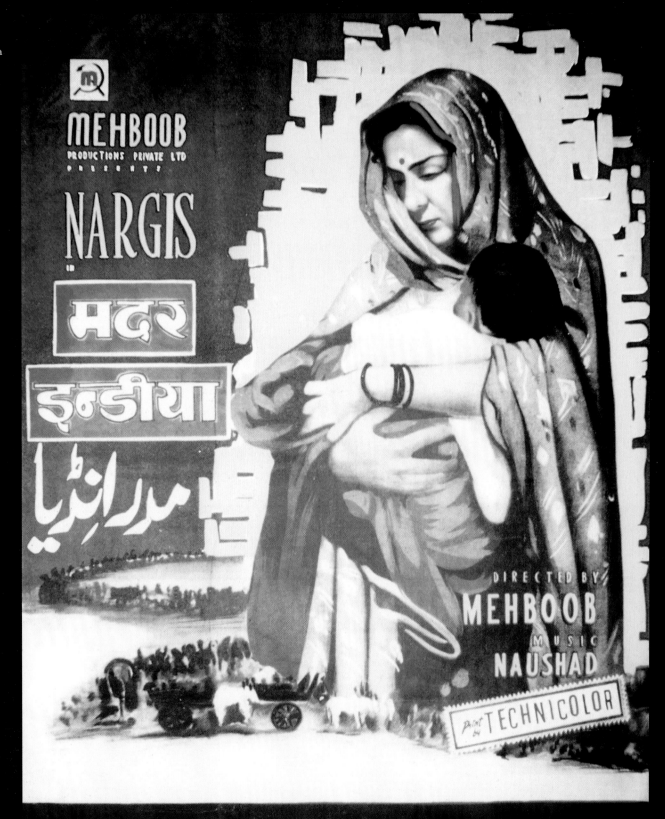

Posters of **PYAASA** and
KAAGAZ KE PHOOL.

Posters of **PYAASA** and
KAAGAZ KE PHOOL.

Prime Minister Jawahar Lal
Nehru with Suraiya.
The first Prime Minister of
India accepted the popular
impact of films and took
steps to promote good
cinema.

music as a cinematic idiom. No other film-maker in India has used songs so effectively to heighten climax as Guru Dutt did in *Pyaasa* or *Kaagaz ke Phool* (1959). His poetic tempera-ment and his training as a dancer helped him to create visual impact with immense dexterity and subtlety.

The early 1960s were marked by the death of the three great pillars of the Golden period – Mehboob, Guru Dutt and Bimal Roy. Guru Dutt died prematurely (allegedly committing suicide at the age of thirty-nine) while both Mehboob and Bimal Roy passed away in their early sixties. All three reached a high level of maturity and creativity in their works. Had they lived longer, Bollywood would have been richer and more versatile.

Promoting Film Culture

A few years after independence, Prime Minister Jawahar Lal Nehru's government took steps to promote cinema at a national level. In 1951 the Report of the Film Enquiry Committee urged the creation of institutions to promote films and train a new generation of filmmakers. The result was the formation of the Film Finance Corporation (FFC) in 1960 and the founding, the following year, of the

Film and Television Institute of India (FTII), located in the historic building of Prabhat Studio, Pune. Another positive step had been the holding in 1952 of the First International Film Festival of India, which gave Indian filmmakers direct exposure to world cinema. Nehru said during a seminar at New Delhi in 1955 that the impact of films was 'greater than the influence of newspapers and books all combined'. His statement was symptomatic of independent India's recognition of the vital importance of cinema. It also marked a clear shift from the thinking of leaders like Mahatma Gandhi, who seemed to have a rather negative perception of films.

1960s – Spillover of Excellence & the Beginning of the Slide

The decade got off to an excellent start with K. Asif's super classic *Mughal-e-Azam* (1960) which can easily be adjudged the best period film of India. Although a historical fiction, *Mughal-e-Azam* is a real cinematic feat of independent India and a true classic of the century in terms of grandeur and sheer spectacle. Its director and producer was an ordinary man, with no formal education, from Etawah, Uttar Pradesh. Yet he had the

KAAGAZ KE PHOOL

Guru Dutt acted in and directed this film. His most ambitious film, it bombed at the box-office, though later proved to be a classic. Discouraged by the initial failure of this film, Guru Dutt retired from directing.

Posters of Vijay Anand's
JOHNY MERA NAAM,
JEWEL THIEF and GUIDE.

creativity and the vision to make a *magnum opus*. The film brought the best out of three legends – Prithviraj Kapoor (Akbar), Madhubala (Anarkali) and Dilip Kumar (Salim). Conceived as early as 1943, *Mughal-e-Azam* is one of the costliest films ever made in India.

It was during this decade that Vijay Anand broke new ground in filmmaking. Films such as *Kala Bazar* (1960), *Hum Dono* (1961) and *Tere Ghar Ke Samne* (1963) made his brother Dev Anand a smart, lovable and believable character. They facilitated his flowering as a matinee idol – in spite of his highly stylized dialogue delivery and a unique dress and headgear (he would often wear a hat!). *Guide* is Vijay Anand's pinnacle as a filmmaker. It is also undoubtedly one of the best films of Indian cinema. 'I built this film brick by brick. It was my interpretation of Raju Guide's character. I did not even rigidly follow the novel', Vijay Anand recalls. All the songs with S.D. Burman's music were thematically placed. The film proved most rewarding for both Dev Anand and Waheeda Rehman. Vijay Anand built up his credentials as a skilful creator of slick entertainment through a string of successful films: *Jewel Thief* (1965), *Teesri Manzil* (1966) and *Johny Mera Naam* (1970)

(the biggest grosser up to the making of *Sholay*, 1975).

In the period that followed, a definite shift towards flamboyance became visible. Cinema gradually started moving away from the earthy, native social subjects of films like *Do Bigha Zamin*, *Humlog*, *Mother India* and *Pyaasa* to pure entertaining fun-loving films like *Jab Pyar Kisi Se Hota Hai* (1961), *Phir Wohi Dil Laya Hoon* (1963) and *Ayee Milan Ki Bela* (1964). In a way, this was a natural response to the rapid urbanization that had started changing society, bringing an inclination towards western values. The generation born after independence also did not share the social concerns of the previous generation.

Gradually, a change also seeped into music. Beat began to replace melody and sentimental nonsense rhymes began to take the place of true poetry. Not all the change was negative. O.P. Nayyar's experiments with western beat created new lilt and pace. *Kashmir ki Kali* (1964) was a landmark: together with the popular numbers of Shanker-Jaikishen in *Junglee* (1961), *Janwar* (1965) and *Professor* (1962), it set the scene for the emergence of the cult of Shammi Kapoor.

As films began to move away from social

Filmmaker Vijay Anand.
Vijay Anand was the most
versatile and creative
filmmaker of the 1960s
whose films appealed to all
classes.

Posters of **DIL DEKE DEKHO** and **JANE ANJANE**.

reality, there was a sea change in audience tastes. A new generation of viewers started idolizing the pranks and the tomfoolery of actors such as Shammi Kapoor and Jeetendra. Male leads no longer fought for land or justice for the poor. Quite a few of them wore glamorous western clothes, played the piano to win the heart of their lady love, and lived in luxurious mansions that would put royalty to shame. New trends were being tried, such as filming abroad. Attractive foreign locations had their share in the huge box-office successes of Raj Kapoor's *Sangam* and Ramanand Sagar's *Aankhen* (1968). That cinema was being trivialized was even apparent from film titles such as *An Evening in Paris* (1967) and *Love in Tokyo* (1966). The former is best remembered for the way Sharmila Tagore was shown in a bikini.

Shakti Samanta's films introduced a new element, a sobering influence. His *Aradhana* (1969), launched a new star with an extremely naïve image – Rajesh Khanna – who then rose like a meteor through his films like *Kati Patang* (1970)*, Amar Prem* (1971) and *Anurodh* (1977)*.*

The 1960s also saw sparkling works such as *Teesri Kasam* by Basu Bhattacharya – Bimal Roy's protégé – and *Sanghursh* (1969) by H.S.

Rawail. *Teesri Kasam,* based on a story by the Hindi writer, Phanishwar Nath Renu, had excellent photography and extracted a very strong performance from Raj Kapoor. Rawail's *Sanghursh* was a powerful drama about nineteenth-century thugs whose dialogues were by Gulzar.

Towards the end of the 1960s, some thinkers, writers and discerning film-lovers were beginning to be unhappy about cinema. They wanted films to retain their dignity, to refuse wholesale co-option by commercial interests. No one knew what the 1970s had in store.

Reaction against Slide – Rise of Parallel/ New Cinema

The increasingly desperate search for a formula for box-office success polarized public opinion and triggered a degeneration of audience taste. To stem the decline, the FFC offered to fund filmmakers with good scripts. Strangely enough, the challenge to make better cinema in Hindi was first picked up by a renowned Bengali filmmaker Mrinal Sen. The result was *Bhuwan Shome* (1969) – a trend-setter of the 'new cinema' genre and a big commercial success. There were others too.

ARADHANA

Rajesh Khanna and
Sharmila Tagore. A series of
box office successes made
Rajesh Khanna the
heart- throb of an entire
generation and created
Bollywood's first super star.

JUNGLEE

Shammi Kapoor and Saira
Banu. This is still regarded
as a cult film due to Shammi
Kapoor's youthful and
rebellious performance.

ANKUR
Shabana Azmi and Anant
Nag. The director of Ankur,
Shyam Benegal, was one of
the pioneers of new cinema
in Hindi.

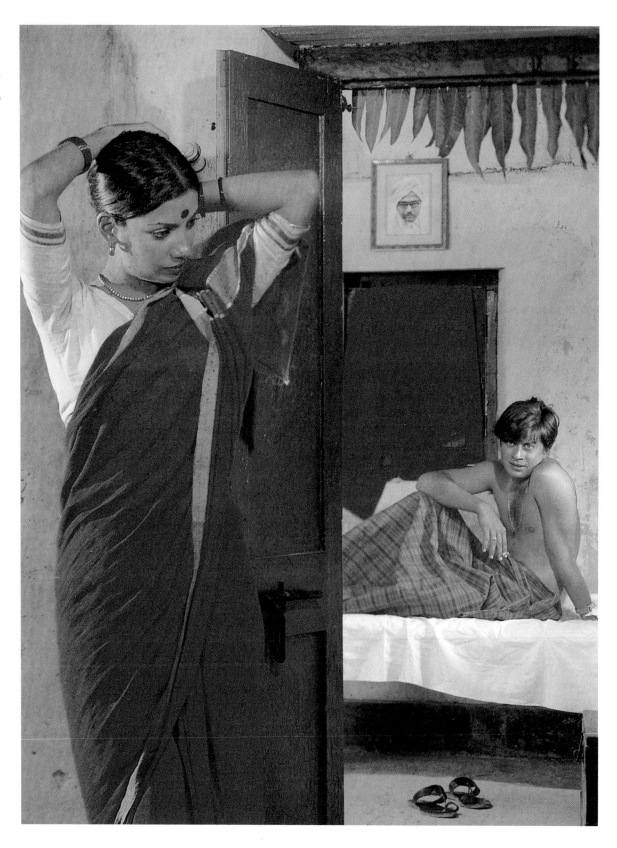

M. S. Sathyu, a filmmaker from Karnataka, made a bold film *Garam Hawa* (1973), on a taboo subject – Hindu-Muslim bad blood. After a long career in advertising films, Shyam Benegal made *Ankur* (1974), a film that became a symbol of 'new cinema'. Similarly, another creative man with vision – Saeed Akhtar Mirza – left a lucrative job in advertising and joined the FTII.

By the end of the 1970s, 'new cinema' had become a movement. Through his trilogy *Ankur, Manthan* (1976) and *Nishant* (1975), Shyam Benegal explored the remnants of feudalism and the struggle of the common man against social injustice. It was Benegal who discovered such versatile talents as Shabana Azmi *(Ankur)* and Smita Patil and Naseeruddin Shah *(Nishant)*. In Govind Nihalani's *Aakrosh* (1980), audiences were moved to wrath along with Lahanya Bhikhu (played by Om Puri), when he discovers that a group of politicians has raped and murdered his wife Nagi (Smita Patil). 'New cinema' bloomed with filmmakers like Saeed Akhtar Mirza *(Albert Pinto Ko Gussa Kyon Ata Hai)*, Ketan Mehta *(Bhavni Bhavai,* 1980), Kumar Shahani *(Tarang,* 1984) and Mani Kaul *(Uski Roti,* 1969).

1970s – Creating A New Myth: Amitabh Bachchan

In Bollywood, the1970s began on an eventful note. In *Aradhana*, Rajesh Khanna appeared to strike a universal chord with his smile, the way he nodded. Almost the whole of the nation's youth were dressing like him. Columnists and critics started calling him the first superstar of India. Young girls were even more adventurous. They wrote love letters to him using their own blood in the place of ink. This was the moment Hrishikesh Mukherjee chose to release *Anand* (1970), a film that set the whole nation crying. Rajesh Khanna (Anand) who knows he will die, looks at the world with a smile and everyone loves him. *Anand* was also Amitabh Bachchan's first appearance as a serious, almost sullen-looking but conscientious doctor (Bhaskar), who thinks the world is full of misery and there is nothing one can do about it. Amitabh's powerful performance was noticed.

Hrishikesh Mukherjee's cinema reflected decency, courage and sentiments of the common man. He did not believe in epics and blockbusters and never made them. His themes touched decent ordinary middle-class people who believed in certain values. His

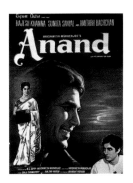

Posters of **ALBERT PINTO KO GUSSA KYOON AATA HAI** and **ANAND**.

AANDHI

Suchitra Sen. Gulzar, the
director, was attending the
Moscow Film Festival with
Aandhi. He got a call from
Indian authorities: Send the
prints back. Aandhi has
been banned!

ANHONEE

Sanjeev Kumar, acknowledged
as one of the finest actors of
Bollywood.

Satyakam (1970) was quite a landmark. Inspired by a real story, it was a simple film about how a sense of honesty and duty was being lost after independence, isolating those who mattered. It was played very sensitively by Dharmendra. Mukherjee also excelled in light-hearted clean features such as *Budha Mil Gaya* (1971), *Chupke Chupke* (1975) and *Golmal* (1979). Amitabh Bachchan and Jaya Bhaduri had their best roles from Mukherjee.

Another filmmaker who made an impact was Gulzar. Being a poet, his cinema had a different feel. His *Mausam* (1975), *Khushboo* (1975) and *Kinara* (1977) created a new class of films, romantic but understated, bold but not loud. His best came in *Aandhi* (1975), a feminist film that made stars of Sanjeev Kumar and Suchitra Sen. It was quite rare for cinema to make a political comment at that time. Parallels were drawn between the life of the Prime Minister, Indira Gandhi, and the leading lady, resulting in a brief ban on the film. Gulzar's legendary status is due to his hold over more than one element of filmmaking: his mastery of lyrics, dialogue-writing and scripts.

But the biggest phenomenon of 1970s

1 4

N. C. SIPPY
PRESENTS
UTTAM
Chitra's

mere apne

EASTMAN COLOR

WRITTEN & DIRECTED BY
GULZAR

MUSIC
SALIL CHOWDHURY

PRODUCED BY
ROMU N. SIPPY & RAJ N. SIPPY

LAL PATTHAR
Raaj Kumar and Hema
Malini. Raaj Kumar was a
noted character actor with
a distinct touch of class. His
aristocratic style of
dialogue delivery was
imitated by millions.

NAMAK HALAL.
Smita Patil and Amitabh
Bachchan. The film remains
one of Prakash Mehra's
biggest hits.

Posters of **ZANJEER** and
SHOLAY.

Bollywood was Amitabh Bachchan. Nationally it was a period of political upheavals and increasing corruption in political and public life. At this juncture, Amitabh's unusual appearance and look of struggling, signalled to people that he was one of them – an ordinary police officer, or a slum dweller who was making it big, so they could too. Amitabh was a myth in the making.

Amitabh's career was lifted by Prakash Mehra's *Zanjeer* (1973), in which he plays a police officer who takes the law into his own hands to avenge the murder of his parents. Mehra's other big hit was *Muqaddar Ka Sikandar* (1978) where Bachchan plays an underclass doomed loner. His success was repeated in Yash Chopra's *Deewaar* (1975), which had a powerful script by Salim-Javed. In this film his character is developed on the model of Haji Mastan Mirza, a noted Mumbai smuggler, who was a friend of the poor. It was Manmohan Desai's *Amar Akbar Anthony* (1977) that proved the versatility of Amitabh as an actor. He also co-starred with Amjad Khan and Dharmendra, in Ramesh Sippy's epic *Sholay*, the biggest blockbuster of the 1970s (it ran continuously for five years in Mumbai). Many critics hold *Sholay* responsible

for glamorizing violence and opening the floodgates to the senseless gore and mayhem of the 1980s and 1990s.

1980s – Violence & Decline

The decade exhausted Amitabh. Manmohan Desai and Prakash Mehra who had jointly built up his image as an angry young man, lost their touch and their later films resorted to repetition with increased doses of violence. There came a time when Amitabh's films started bombing. Films like Manmohan Desai's *Ganga Jamuna Saraswati* (1988) and Ramesh Sippy's *Akayla* (1991) not only showed a downslide in commercial film standards but also poor judgement on the part of Amitabh as to what kinds of roles he should accept. In spite of being one of the most talented actors, misjudgement in selecting roles was partly responsible for a dip in his career in the 1990s. On the contrary, veteran actor Dilip Kumar and talented actress, Shabana Azmi were able to avoid such a predicament because they were extremely choosy.

A few filmmakers, like Punkaj Parasher and Vidhu Vinod Chopra, did try to break new ground in cinema with their early films.

Poster of **UMRAO JAAN**.

ARDH SATYA
Om Puri depicting police
brutality in forcing a
confession from a suspect.
The film had an immense
impact on commercial
cinema and put filmmaker
Govind Nihalani under
pressure to make other
films of similar genre.

Structurally, Chopra's *Parinda* (1989) was
stunning, with a chilling murder sequence
quite new to Hindi cinema. But ironically,
these films did not meet with an enthusiastic
audience response.

Gradually, mainstream commercial Hindi
cinema of the 1980s lost its traditional audience. The arrival of video and television serials
was partly responsible. Barring a few excep-
tions, such as Muzaffar Ali's classic *Umrao
Jaan* (1981) and Mahesh Bhatt's powerful
Saaransh (1984), films in general became
increasingly bereft of content. Govind
Nihalani's *Ardh Satya* (1983), was a powerful
work, that exposed the nexus between the
politician and the police. However, there was
no denying that by and large, good cinema
was being sucked in by commercial considera-

tions. The nadir seemed to have been reached
by the 1990s. The only antidote to the cycle of
violence towards the end of 1980s was young
Sooraj Barjatya's debut film, *Maine Pyar Kiya*
(1989), a trend-setting teenage love saga.

**1990s – Violence with Titillation: Complete
Crisis of Content**
By the early 1990s, by and large, Bollywood
had come full circle. A growing crisis of
content had fostered an increased reliance on
violence, sex and titillation. The popularity
that cinema had enjoyed from the 1950s to the
1970s was almost lost. Cinema audiences now
consisted mainly of young people and the
easily pleased, who came seeking fun. Film
song-and-dance sequences degenerated into
group drills. Actors and actresses were

PHOOL AUR KAANTE
Ajay Devgan. In the 1980s
and 1990s violence was
increasingly glamorized.

reduced to emoting through pelvic, hip and
bosom thrusts and gyrations, singing bawdy
songs and delivering hollow, or cheap repetitive dialogues *ad nauseam*. It simply did not
seem the medium that once belonged to filmmakers like Bimal Roy and Mehboob.

As a filmmaker, David Dhawan became a
sure brand of box-office success with Govinda
and Karisma Kapoor as a lead pair. The positive side of the 1990s was the entry of Ram
Gopal Verma and Mani Ratnam into
Bollywood. Both made good films but played
safe by trying to achieve cinematic excellence
within the parameters of commercial cinema.
Ratnam's *Bombay* (1995) documents the
Hindu Muslim divide and Verma's *Satya* (1998)
is a classic that mirrors Mumbai's ruthless

world of crime. The post-Ratnam young Turks
like Karan Johar and Aaditya Chopra are solely
dedicated to a feel-good, romantic story-
telling with a lot of gloss and very little
substance. Their films are tailored to suit the
cell phone flashing new generation. In Aaditya
Chopra's *Mohabbatein* (2000), the glamorous
Gurukul students eat Pringles and dress up
like London schoolboys. Another young
talented filmmaker to emerge is Sanjay Leela
Bhansali, but his films also try to woo the
urban audience or South Asians settled
abroad. A new crop of Bollywood filmmakers
is emerging. Meghna Gulzar, the daughter of
veteran lyricist/filmmaker, Gulzar, is ready
with her debut film, *Filhaal* (2001) that
explores friendship and love. Filmmaker

MAACHIS

Violence is an important theme in this film, dealing with the rise of terrorism during the separatist movement in Punjab. An innocent family is persecuted by the police and turns to terrorism.

DIL TO PAGAL HAI

Shah Rukh Khan and Madhuri Dixit. This was Yash Chopra's biggest commercial success in the 1990s, with top Bollywood stars and many song-and-dance numbers.

Farhan Akhtar, son of the renowned screen-play writer, Javed Akhtar has also raised expectations.

The Millennium Scenario

Bollywood is shifting audience focus. It is reaching out to the Non-Resident Indians (NRIs). But will it win over the western audience too? Some believe that it is very difficult and premature to venture a guess. Undoubtedly, some films have recently done well abroad. But many ambitious Bollywood ventures are bombing both at home and abroad. The entire market is in a state of flux. Technical excellence has no doubt been hitting a new high.The first five minutes of Rakesh Mehra's *Aks* (2001) for instance, make you feel you are watching a Hollywood film. But the content eventually brings it down.

Indophiles would like to see Bollywood taking over the West, like Indian curry has managed to do. It can be argued that India has the potential. But after nearly thirty years of filmmaking, Shyam Benegal, for one, does not have any illusions: 'Hollywood cannot be challenged at this stage for the simple reason that they have vast infrastructure both of exhibition and distribution and the revenue receipts

that they earn are astronomical compared to Indian cinema.'

It is true that to go international, Bollywood films have to rise above naïvety. One way to extend the Indian film market is to subtitle them, but that has already started. 'We have not yet got the Anglo-Saxon markets. To get that market you have got to make films that they consider entertaining. At the moment our films appear to them to be somewhat naïve, not always believable. Our subject matter, our characterization, and our story-telling will have to have greater depth. If I see that happening at all, it's happening very, very slowly', says Benegal.

Play on... The Music

The music in **MUGHAL-E-AZAM** marked the peak of Naushad's career; after making the film, he said that he had no more to offer creatively; it took him years to return to his work.

NAYADAUR
Vyjayanthimala dancing to O.P. Nayyar's tune. His music was the binding force of this B.R. Chopra classic.

Dilip Kumar and Waheeda
Rehman in **RAM AUR
SHYAM**. The film is
remembered for
Naushad's music.

This could happen in any town in India. Some eunuchs gather in front of a house, singing and dancing to the beat of a *dholak* (Indian drum)... and you suddenly know that a baby has been born in that house. The child is brought out. Turn by turn, all the eunuchs take it in their arms and sing blessings into its ears. The baby is baptized by music.

This is the point from which music starts in an Indian life...

The baby grows up, listening to musical *bhajans* (Hindu religious songs) and the folk-lore of different regions in all the ceremonies that it goes through – the *Annaprasan* (first ceremonial feeding of grain) ceremony, *Janeo* (sacred thread) ceremony and *Mundan* (head shaving) ceremony, among others. All these are conducted musically with hymns, *bhajans*, *qawwalis* (Sufi devotional music) and family singing. The *dholak* is the most familiar sound for any child growing up. The curd-seller on the street, the milkman coming home, even the washer-men at the *dhobi ghat*, or the rice-beating women in the courtyard, all sing as they go about their business. All these cameos are familiar to every cine-goer in India. They are in the entire environment, ready to be absorbed.

In the villages, people sing for the rains to arrive: *Allah megh de, megh de, paani de...* (God, give us clouds, give us clouds... S.D. Burman, *Guide*). When the rains arrive, they sing: *Hariyaala Saawan dhol bajaata aaya...* (Dancing to the beat of the drum comes the green month of August... Salil Chowdhury, *Do Bigha Zamin*). Such situations have appeared many a time in films, most recently in *Lagaan* (2001). Then comes the harvest. A recent harvest song is: *Dhol bajne lagaa...* (The *dhol* has begun playing... A.R. Rahman, *Virasat,* 1997).

In addition to the seasons, there are also many festivals in India, each with its own songs and rituals that keep bouncing into our films. You play *Holi* (festival of colours), and there are umpteen number of songs for it. You fly a kite on *Sankranti*, and there are songs for it: *Chali chali re patang meri chali re...* (Here goes my kite, here it goes...) Come *Raksha Bandhan* (an Indian festival), and every sister recalls: *Bhaiya mere, raakhi ke bandhan ko nibhaana...* (Oh my brother! Break not the bonds of my raakhi...).

These festivals resonate in our music in an unending cycle. They keep circulating with

Aruna Irani in a dance
number from Nasir
Hussain's **CARAVAN**.

Sohrab Modi's **MIRZA GHALIB**. Ghulam Mohammed's music and Shakeel Badayuni's lyrics turned this film into an all-time classic.

fresh sounds and energy in our cinema, time after time….

Music is also an essential part of Indian cinema due to the tradition of the narrative style. The great epics – the *Ramayana* and the *Mahabharata* – were both written in verse and memorized by singing through the ages. In addition, the tradition of Indian classical music is such that the *raagas* (a combination of notes) also narrate the state of mind, musically, with the help of very brief phrases of verse. It is only in films that these verses become elongated lyrics.

This kind of emotional indulgence is yet another reason for long-drawn and lengthy films. Perhaps, too, it relates to the Indian pace of life, in contrast to that of the West. The pace of the music of every culture is always related to its pace of life.

Some film songs have become synonymous with certain ceremonies. They have almost replaced the folk songs or become a part of them: *Gore gore haathon mein mehendi laga ke*… (With henna decorating your fair hands…) is bound to be heard in every marriage. As is: *Chhod babul ka ghar, aaj pi ke nagar, mohe jaana pada*… (Leaving behind my father's home, I'm bound to go today to my beloved's abode…) and *Babul mora, neyhar chhooto hi jaaye*…(My father, I'm leaving behind the place I was born…)

Naushad has undoubtedly given us the most songs which have become part of the Indian milieu. Nor can we forget his song of the bullock-carts from *Mother India* – *Gaadi waale, gaadi dheere haank re*… (Oh Bullock - cart driver! Goad the bullocks gently to move on!…) And there are many others, from Vasant Desai's *Jeevan se lambe hain bandhoo, ye jeevan ke raaste*… (Longer than Life itself, my friend, seems the journey of life…) in *Aashirwad* (Blessings, 1968), to Shankar-

A dance sequence from
ACHCHUT KANYA, made
in 1936; the Golden Age of
music was to follow.

Rishi Kapoor and Sridevi in
BANJARA, dancing to the
beats of Bhangra.

Filmmaker and lyricist,
Gulzar.

Jaikishen's *Chitthian ho tau har koi baanche, bhaag na baanche koe…* (Everyone can read if it is a letter, but inscrutable are the ways of fate…) in Basu Bhattacharya's *Teesri Kasam* (1966).

The boatman's song existed in old New Theatre films and kept appearing and re-appearing right up to composer Roshan's *Taal mile nadi ke jal mein…* (The lake merges into the river…)*, S.D. Burman's *O re manjhi…* (O! Boatman…) and R.D. Burman's *O manjhi re…*

In fact Hindi film music has played a significant role in the integration of folk music in India. Cinema has brought folk music from different regions into the mainstream. Culturally and musically, every region has a very distinct style of its own. Punjab, for example, stands out for its *Bhangra* (Punjabi

folk dance) numbers. This style has a fast beat and is full of energy. It is generally performed along with a community dance, especially during harvest time. *Gidda* and *Kikli* are the other two styles, which are feminine in character, though males also participate. In some of the recent films of Yash Chopra, these have been considerably utilized.

Raj Kapoor's film *Jagte Raho* (1956) had a *Bhangra* number – '*Main koi jhooth boliya*' (Have I told a lie?) – which once ruled the pop charts.

Goa is identified by its Konkani culture, with a dominant Portuguese influence resulting from a four-hundred-year colonization. Songs of the Goan fisher-folk have a distinct style. These songs appear recurrently in a number of Hindi films that have Mumbai

and the sea as the background. Raj Kapoor has used them effectively in *Bobby* (1973). That famous song in *Bobby*, '*Jhoot bole kawwa kaate…*' (The crow will peck you if you lie…), was also instrumental in introducing a very glamorous heroine to Hindi Cinema.

The 'boatman's songs' of the East are also famous, and are called *Bhaatiyali* songs in the colloquial language of that region. S.D. Burman's *O re Manjhi* (O Boatman!), from the film *Sujata* (1959), is a very memorable example. Again, in *Bandini* (1963), the composer used two more songs in the *Bhaatiyali* style – *O re manjhi le chal paar…*

(O boatman, take me across…) and *O jaanewale ho sakey to laut ke aana…* (O traveller, do return if you can…).

The Rajasthani folk songs have been very beautifully rendered by the 'Queen of Melody', Lata Mangeshkar, in films like *Lekin* (1991) and *Rudaali* (1993). These are the timeless numbers of Indian film music.

Gujarat and Maharashtra have made an ample contribution to the mainstream with their folk songs and sound styles. Their musical instruments also hold an important distinction. The *Dandiya* numbers are known for their swaying style of composition and

Smita Patil gives a stunning start to Shyam Benegal's **BHUMIKA**.

The music in V. Shantaram's **AADMI** was composed by Master Krishnarao who was both an actor and a great music director of the 1930s and 1940s.

colourful dances. The two wooden sticks held by the dancers are the hallmark of *Dandiya*. Similarly, the *Lavni* is the most exotic dance of Maharashtra. This style of music, with variations and improvizations, has also been used by composers. A young composer like Vishal Bhardwaj has used it effectively in *Hu Tu Tu* (1999) – *Neem ke tale se nikla*… (The moon has come out from under the branches of the neem tree…)

These and a number of other styles have merged into mainstream Indian music and enriched it immensely. This also brings about a cultural integration and a pleasant musical exchange between people of different regions. Music is a great unifying factor and generates social harmony among people. Indian film music has made an immense contribution to this end.

Another common tradition since the poems and songs of our saints and Sufis is the *Faqir* song, popularly called the *baoul* ballads. This device was used in films for thematic enhancement. A very old traditional song of the Sufis has a brilliant modern version by A.R. Rahman: *Chal chhaiyan chhaiyan*… (Come to the shade, the shade…) in Mani Ratnam's *Dil Se* (1998).

A.R. Rahman, in particular, must be noted as having reached a new milestone in Indian film music. He has internationalized Indian music with new sounds but, unlike most composers of our times, he has kept the traditional strain intact. His work is modern, innovative and Indian in essence. His patriotic number *Ma tujhe salaam*… (Salutations to you, My Motherland…) is a significant addition to our national songs.

To understand the beginning of music in cinema it is important to look at how it entered the cinema halls. In front of the movie screen there used to be a music pit where musicians would sit and provide 'live' music for the visuals of the film, or bioscope as it was then called. This was during the 'Silent Era'. The 'live' music of *sarangi*, *tabla* and *harmonium* (piano and violin in the case of English films), played very loudly, would drown out the sounds of not only the noisy film projectors, but also the calls of roaming hawkers selling *paan-beedi* and lemon-soda… The audience would send requests for their favourite songs, regardless of the visuals and situations on screen!

This was the period when light-classical and semi-classical numbers flourished.

Naseeruddin Shah and
Sonam performing a dance
routine in Rajiv Rai's
TRIDEV. The music
composer was Kalyanji
Anandji.

JOHNY MERA NAAM
Dev Anand and Hema Malini
The film's songs based on
Kalyanji Anandji music and
Rajender Krishan and
Indivar's catchy lyrics
became a rage in the 1970s.

The dream sequence in Raj
Kapoor's **AWARA**.

The *gutt* (pace) was fast and loud. Our folk songs were rejuvenated too – solo and group numbers, helped by musicians, by the *masterji*, the instructor; and by the *munshi*, who would throw out impromptu dialogue to accompany the scene and sometimes excite the audience with expletives urging the hero to go on hitting the villain and turn him into a pulp! Cinema was a live show then.

A few songs like those of *Holi* or *Vidai* (Parting) or *Rukhsati* (Farewell) had a great effect on the audience, and they would request the same song for the same scene, in every show. Thus emerged song situations in films.

The more enterprising exhibitors, who were also the distributors, began to hire the services of *kavis* (poets) to add fresh, exciting lines and put more emotion in the song, and of *masterji* to give the music more punch. Thus emerged the lyricist and the music director.

Then talkies arrived in 1931, followed by playback singing in 1935, and film music became more durable. It was not long before the *Kaala tawa* (78rpm records) arrived on the scene. The music of the film began to step out of the confines of the theatre. Imagine what a revolution it must have been – a song could be heard outdoors, without the presence of a singer. Just a needle to prick a disc and a human voice could be heard singing! People were amazed. Now film music had reached the streets, especially through the wheel-carts that advertised films.

Songs became an effective draw for films, building up to the frenzy of today. Though attached to the story's narrative, music always had an independent identity. Even now, a film may flop and its music be a hit, or vice-versa. Today, most of a film's returns come from its music. Film music is at the matured age of seventy years, and is growing ever more youthful.

Before playback was introduced in the early talkies, singing artistes were hired for the roles. The musicians had to move around with the artistes, hidden from the camera lens. Thus the musical instruments were confined to the minimum, say the *sarangi*, *tabla* and *manjira* (cymbal). The harmonium was avoided for recording unless it was essential to the scene. The singing voice remained the prime concern.

W.M. Khan was the first singing hero of the first talkie, *Alam Ara* (1931). His song *De de Khuda ke naam pe...* (Give, give, in the name

The strength of the music in B.R. Chopra's **NAYA DAUR**, was not only in the composition of tunes, but also in the poetic and socially relevant lyrics of Sahir Ludhianvi.

The magic in Hrishikesh Mukherjee's **ANARI** was created by two people - the lyricist, Shailendra and the music director, Shankar-Jaikishen.

of God…) became very famous. But there was no mention of a music director in the credits of the film. The songs were probably picked up from other sources.

In 1935, Debaki Bose introduced playback in his film *Chandidas*. It opened the floodgates for music in films. The instruments multiplied tenfold – now the violin, *pakhawaj*, *jal-tarang*, *sitar* and *rabab* could be heard in the songs. Even the number of songs in films increased, until the musical length outgrew the length of the spoken word. Films such as *Inder Sabha* (1956) and *Taj Mahal* (1963) are cases in point.

The early sources of film music were classical scores and folklore. The subjects were also rural, some drawn from mythology and some from folk theatre. However, as the developing cities began making their impact on our cultural milieu and day to day life, the *Shehri Babu* (or city dweller) became a common character in our narrative, as did the *Vilayati* – the one who returned from overseas. The musical compositions began to change accordingly. A modern song meant more use of the piano, which sounded distinctly foreign. A variant of the violin – called the *behula* – was already present among Indian instruments.

Ravan-hattha is another form, popular in Rajasthan.

The national movement for independence impacted on our films and music simultaneously. Songs like *Chal chal re naujawan…* (Move forward, young man!…) and *Door hato ey duniyavalon…* (Move off, you outsiders, India belongs to us…) set the new trend in patriotic songs with a marching beat. After the Second World War, there was a shift of the population to urban areas. The language of the dialogues and lyrics also changed. *Avadhi* and *Bhojpuri* (two regional dialects of Hindi) began receding, while *Khari boli* (Standard Hindi) took their place. However, being the language of the theatre, Urdu remained dominant in film dialogue and lyrics, with *ghazals* being a popular lyrical form.

Naushad became the leading music composer, but he continued to base his compositions on Indian classical and folk music till others such as C. Ramchandra appeared with their early beat-dominated musical compositions.

Noor Jahan and Mohammad Rafi were the dominant voices and K.L. Saigal was a class apart. All three grew to the stature of legends in the Indian film music scene. A future

Dharmendra and Nutan in Bimal Roy's classic **BANDINI**; the credit for this film's success goes equally to the veteran S.D. Burman for his earthy, haunting songs.

Opposite page

MADHUMATI, a Bimal Roy
film, was a big commercial
success because it
combined a strong story
by legendary Bengali
filmmaker, Ritwik Ghatak,
with lilting folk music by
Salil Chowdhury and lyrics
by Shailendra.

Right

R.D. Burman's music was at
its best in Gulzar's
AANDHI.

legend, singer Lata Mangeshkar, had just
appeared on the horizon.

Then came 1947. Partition re-shuffled the
entire population and along with it, the film
and music industry. Bombay, (now Mumbai),
became with Bollywood the biggest
film-producing centre. Lahore was totally
shattered while Calcutta was reduced to
making regional films, rather than mainstream
Hindustani cinema. Joining the film directors,
some very prominent music directors shifted
to Bombay – S.D. Burman, Hemant Kumar, Salil
Chowdhury among them. Even Ravi Shankar
joined films to provide music for K.A. Abbas's
Dharti Ke Lal (1946) and later Hrishikesh
Mukherjee's *Anuradha* (1960), as well as
Satyajit Ray's *Pather Panchali* (1955).

This was the Golden Period of the 1950s
and 1960s, the longest spell of melody in Hindi
film music. Ironically, socially and politically,
it was also the most disturbed period after
Partition. A chaotic state of unemployment
prevailed in the country, there was an influx
of refugees from the northeast and northwest,
and there were two wars with Pakistan. The
refugees were not yet settled, their wounds
of Partition were still fresh.

The films and film music of the time did the

job of soothing the soul. For two decades, not a
single film was made on the horror of Partition,
save one – *Lahore* (1949) – which was a mere
boy-girl love story.

There was romance in films and melody
in music. The dreams were alive. India had
begun to rebuild its social structure. The entire
melody of film music was providing the background score for the Nation. The hopes for the
future were very, very high.

Hailing from the state of Tripura, the
genius of S.D. Burman provided the richest of
folk music from the eastern region. Hemant
Kumar, in *Rabindra Sangeet* (Tagorean music),
made magic with his voice. Still, Salil
Chowdhury probably represented the best
of east and west fusion, being fluent in both.
He adapted Russian, Polish and other East
European folk music for Indian films such
as *Do Bigha Zamin* and *Madhumati* (1958).

This does not undermine the contribution
of the maestros who were already established
in Bombay. Among them were names such
as R.C. Boral, Roshan, Madan Mohan, Sajjad,
Khayyam, Vasant Desai, Shankar-Jaikishen,
Jaidev and of course Naushad as well as
C. Ramchandra and O.P. Nayyar. Each had his
respective phases of success and popularity,

though C. Ramchandra and O.P. Nayyar, with their innovative styles, reigned supreme in beat-dominated melodies.

C. Ramchandra was remarkable for introducing a distinct western beat. His song *Gore gore, O banke chhore*… (O fair, brave lad, do pass down my lane…) was one of the earliest street hits, and was responsible for Bhagwan Dada's Rumba-Samba dance numbers. O.P. Nayyar, of course, was the cherry on top of the 'beat-music' in Hindi films. Another remarkable music director R.D. Burman, is well known for his melodious compositions as well as beat. Voice always dominated his compositions. He himself was a good singer, though Kishore Kumar remained his favourite.

Although songs carry the stamp of their composers, film music in India has also been influenced by its filmmakers. The film director often dominates and influences the composer. The choice of songs becomes very subjective and the composer has little option but to provide whatever the director or producer of the film demands. The films of V. Shantaram, for example, have a distinct flavour of music and even verse. The music of the duo Shankar-Jaikishen has never been the same outside Raj

Kapoor's films, which were known for their musical excellence. B.R. Chopra and Yash Chopra, under the banner of B.R. Films, provided a different brand of Urdu poetry, which was mostly created by music director Ravi and poet Sahir Ludhianvi. However, after Yash Chopra parted from his brother, the music of his banner – Yashraj Films – also changed and lost its identity.

R.D. Burman's work in my films always stood apart from the rest of his creative repertoire. All these filmmakers employed lyrics and melody as an idiom of the film narrative that has made Indian cinema unique in the world.

But as the 1960s faded into the 1970s, the Golden Era of Melody also started melting

Salman Khan and Rani
Mukherjee sing a romantic
duet in the backdrop of the
Swiss Alps.

Salman Khan and Rani
Mukherjee sing a romantic
duet in the backdrop of the
Swiss Alps.

away. The social and political culture had
begun to change. 1971 saw the third war
with Pakistan and the birth of a new country,
Bangladesh on the eastern wing of the
subcontinent. The political disturbances
gathered momentum in Sri Lanka and the
Naxalite Movement caught on in Bengal.
Emergency was declared in India in June
1975. Kashmir was simmering and Punjab
was just about to ignite. All this resulted in
a number of flagrant political assassinations
in and around India, engulfing almost the
whole of South Asia within a decade.

In the 1970s, there was also the Parallel
Cinema of Shyam Benegal, Kumar Shahani
and Mani Kaul, but this had no musical
impact. Then there was the 'Middle-of-the
road Cinema' of Hrishikesh Mukherjee, Gulzar
and Basu Chatterji which was musically quite
enriched. Finally there was the Formula
Cinema, full of clichéd narrative and music.
Film was bound to reflect its times. The hope
of the 1960s was obscured, but lingered for a
while in the 1970s, till total chaos took over.

Like some saner voices on the social scene,
some music composers also held onto their
roots. A new generation had arisen, but with
very weak and fragile stems. Many could not

Preity Zinta and Hrithik Roshan in a famous dance number from Vidhu Vinod Chopra's **MISSION KASHMIR**.

Rani Mukherjee swaying to the rhythms of A.R. Rehman's music in **NAYAK**.

Anil Kapoor and Sridevi
frolicking in the fields in
MR.INDIA

Zeenat Aman and Shashi
Kapoor in **SATYAM
SHIVAM SUNDARAM**,
Raj Kapoor's flight of
imagination with songs
by Anand Bakshi and music
by Laxmikant Pyarelal.

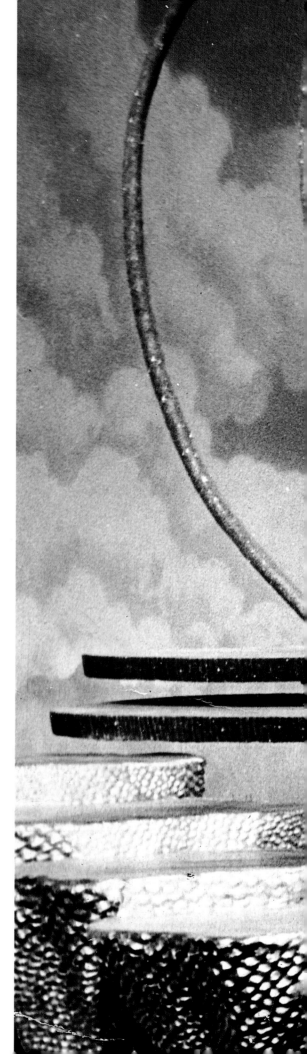

withstand the winds of change – they came
and were blown away. The angry young man
loomed on the horizon, frustration writ large
on the screen. With the disharmony in social
values, corruption became the currency of the
day. Blatant plagiarism began to rule. Thriller
was the key word, the goal, anything that
would sell and be consumed instantly. Fake
currency does not stay in circulation for long.
The disharmony in society was reflected in the
music too. Like all other consumer goods, it
succumbed to the market's demands. Music
became a fast-food joint.

Everything changes. Nothing remains the
same. But inspired lyrics dressed up in good
music never die. They remain the bedrock
of Bollywood excellence. But they owe their
immortality to a few voices. These legends
of the music world are Lata, Asha, Rafi and
Kishore. The most versatile playback singers
for the medium of films, they could mould
their rendering of a song to suit the character
requirement. Rafi, of course, was more than
competent – he sang for the heroes of the
film as well as the cameo characters, say a
comedian, a beggar or even a *sadhu*. His
songs for Johny Walker are memorable. Asha
Bhosle also had a large range. She sang for

the heroine as well as for the cabaret dancer and the 'bad girl'. The other singers mostly confined themselves to singing for the heroes and heroines. Though very popular, they were chosen mainly for their individual styles. Hemant Kumar, Mukesh and Talat Mehmood each had a distinct voice timbre. Lata Mangeshkar, for her effortless singing, can only be compared to Lata Mangeshkar herself. She has no match!

The newer generations have tried to emulate the established, legendary singers and thus remained only copies and failed to make a mark. Plenty of Latas and Rafis have floated in the field. However, it is not only the voice but also how the song is emoted, that counts.

Coming back to the changing times, films were entering the 1990s, hoping to leave the chaos behind. At this time, Pancham, better known as R.D. Burman, son of maestro S.D. Burman, was perhaps the last milestone of melody who held onto his roots.

Laxmikant Pyarelal generated hopes but their music remained an amalgam of many styles, unable to carve a niche of its own. Illayaraja was supremely talented, but could not last in film music for long. Likewise, there

was Hridayanath Mangeshkar, brother of melody queen Lata Mangeshkar. Good souls, for whom the commercial demands of the music world proved too tough to handle.

The 1990s have also faded away. With the new millennium, the thirst for music only appears to have increased. The number of songs in films is on the rise again, dare I say, just like in the past.

Akin to parallel cinema, there is a parallel line of music now: non-film albums. A few giants like the late Nusrat Fateh Ali Khan, Mehndi Hassan, Ghulam Ali and Jagjit Singh have appeared, institutions in themselves. They are already mentioned among the legends of popular music. Here it is the folk music of the Punjab that has made the strongest impact. Malkit Singh of the United Kingdom was perhaps the pioneer, and now Daler Mahendi perhaps rules the roost. I use the word 'perhaps' because the popularity charts change very rapidly these days…! Once again, this genre is also flooded with extreme mediocrity.

We are still thirsty. Very thirsty…

If music quenches the thirst of the soul, play on… please play on…!

Romantic Duets in Contemporary Cinema
left
Sunil Shetty and Kajol.

Karisma Kapoor and Akshay Kumar.

The Classics and Blockbusters

ANARKALI

Bina Roy plays the slave
girl Anarkali, making fiction
greater than truth in this
historical period film.

Bollywood is a dream factory: an institution that never tires of churning out celluloid spectacles, bordering on myth and reality. Its often larger-than-life images enthrall, mesmerize or simply entertain millions across the globe. It packages emotions for pleasure, just as Hollywood does. However, unlike mainstream American films, Bollywood cinema has one particularly stringent recipe for success – repackaging tried and tested thematic elements with new stylistic adventures in song and dance.

Bollywood is a word generally used to describe popular Hindi films produced in Mumbai (formerly called Bombay), but over the years the journalistic term has come to refer to a certain kind of formula. It actually implies a universe of Hindi films marked by an eternal fight between good and evil that derives much from the Indian epics and folk traditions. Thus, most Bollywood films highlight 'idealized' social behaviour and content and rarely disquiet the viewer. Filmmakers and audiences alike are aware of basic twists in narrative, yet a few films – and sometimes entire sections of scripts and the voices of actors – have come to be etched in popular memory for generations. These films are examples of classic cinema that continue to evoke in the audience a certain emotion of identification that transcends barriers of time and space.

Sociology of Classics and Blockbusters

On an average, about 170 Hindi films are made every year, 125 are released in cinema halls, a handful succeed at the box office and barely one or two become real hits. Perhaps this reveals something about Indian audiences and their collective psyche, which can identify films deserving their attention.

Nevertheless, can anyone actually define how a classic film comes about? The 1942 Humphry Bogart-Ingrid Bergman film

DASTAN

Dilip Kumar with Padma
Khanna. Ever versatile and
unaffected by stardom,
Dilip Kumar has inspired
several generations of
actors in the sub-continent.

PURAB AUR PASCHIM

Manoj Kumar's films
carried a liberal dose of
patriotism and the
inevitable triumph of Indian
culture over Western
values.

SATYAM SHIVAM SUNDARAM
Shashi Kapoor and Zeenat Aman in this hit movie directed by Raj Kapoor which illustrates the changing trend of directors using female actresses as sex symbols.

Casablanca (1942) is universally revered by film lovers today, but was initially a low priority film for the Warner Brothers studio. Bogart did not want to act in the film; the director Michael Curtiz began shooting even before the final script was ready and then rushed it through so he could begin his next assignment. No one had any idea that it would become an all-time classic in both an artistic and a commercial sense.

The situation in Bollywood is as unpredictable as that in Hollywood. *Jai Santoshi Ma* (1975), a film based on an obscure religious theme made with a little over Rs. 600,000, grossed Rs. 60.5 million, much to the surprise of trade pundits. Conversely, *Mera Naam Joker* (1970), the *magnum opus* of the celebrated actor-producer-director Raj Kapoor, was rejected by the masses despite having all the essential Bollywood ingredients. It is true that many Bollywood directors have drawn amazing success from Hollywood hits, reworking story-lines to appeal to the Indian heart and mind. However, films that rely on duplicating the content or form of a successful film rarely win critical appreciation. In the last seventy years, more than 28,000 popular Hindi films have been produced, but only three to

MAINE PYAR KIYA

Salman Khan and Mohnish
Behl in director Sooraj
Barjatya's first film. It was a
huge box office success.

BOBBY

Rishi Kapoor and Dimple
Kapadia in a love story that
made teenage rebellion
fashionable.

four dozens can be classified as must-see films
for cinema enthusiasts.

Starcast

Most successful films boast of at least one
star. Familiar faces are an obvious selling point
and generally assure an initial draw to a film.
The star's image and the story-line are
expected to complement each other. Even a
low budget film like *Satya* (1998) banked on a
recognizable female lead, Urmila Matondkar.
Fewer films have become hits with unknown
faces in lead roles. Three films *Bobby* (1973),
Maine Pyar Kiya (*MPK*, 1989) and *Kaho Naa
Pyaar Hai* (*KNPH*, 2000) – all teenage romance
stories – stand out for creating history at the

box-office with previously unknown actors.
Raj Kapoor's son Rishi became a star after
Bobby, and so did scriptwriter Salim's son
Salman Khan, and actor-director-producer
Rakesh Roshan's son Hrithik, following the
mega success of *MPK* and *KNPH*, respectively.
Director Prakash Mehra's action film *Zanjeer*
(1973) helped create for actor Amitabh
Bachchan the image of an angry young man
that turned him into a superstar. Interestingly,
hit films have made new stars out of male
heroes, while female leads have not often
achieved this kind of sudden success.

Music and Dance

Song and dance sequences are the lifeline of a

BHARAT SHAH PRESENTS
RAMGOPAL VERMA'S

satya

the other side of truth

STARRING J.D.CHAKRAVARTHY, URMILA MATONDKAR

SOURAB SHUKLA, MANOJ VAJPAYEE, MAKAN DESHPANDE, GOVIND NAMDEV, PARESH RAWAL,

ADITYA SRIVASTAV, SNEHAL, RAJA MAVANI, SABEER, RAJESH JOSHI, SANJAY MISHRA, SHAFALI

PRODUCER VERMA CORPORATION LTD. EXECUTIVE PRODUCER P. SOMASEKHAR

WRITTEN BY SOURAB SHUKLA, ANURAG KASYAP LYRICS GULZAR MUSIC VISHAL

CINEMATOGRAPHY GERORD HOOPER, MAZHAR HAMRAN EDITING APOORVA-BHANU

CHOREOGRAPHY AHAMAD KHAN ACTION CO-ORDINATOR AMIN GHANI ART DIRECTOR KRISHNA

सत्या

www.satya-the-film.com

Hindi film. They encourage repeat viewing, especially among younger segments of the population. Some directors say that they have a sociological function because in addition to providing entertainment, they give audiences a break without overtly interrupting the narrative flow of the film.

Morals as Themes

A strong story with a moral at the end is necessary in a Bollywood film. Indian cinema has largely survived on the support of the rural and semi-urban masses. Studies show that most Indian audiences do not like major shifts in narrative. They appear to prefer simple good versus evil scenarios, often drawn from the ancient epic of pan-Indian influence, the *Ramayana*. Glorification of the family, individual sacrifice for the sake of others, respect for age and authority, and the long-term futility of crime are themes found in Indian cultural forms throughout history. It is not in the least surprising, then, to see them forming the basis for plots in modern cinema.

Packaging the Story with Believable Characters

Following the epic tradition and to aid viewers

in identifying with narratives, writers have created unusually inspiring characters: a self-respecting woman – *Duniya Na Mane* (1937), a sacrificing mother – *Mother India* (1957), a loving brother – *Ganga Jamuna* (1961), a courtesan with a golden heart – *Pakeezah* (1972), a one-man army determined to avenge social ills in scores of Amitabh Bachchan films and, more recently, a Non-Resident Indian (NRI) steeped in Indian tradition in *Dilwale Dulhaniya Le Jayenge* (1995). The super-hit film *Kismet* (1943) introduced Indian audiences to the 'lost-and-found' brother formula. Since then, writers have developed several plot variants such as sisters separated at birth or in childhood, brothers growing up on different sides of the law, and a son discovering his illegitimacy.

Mixing the Right Formula

A hero's rise through a film reassures audiences in an insecure world. A good film induces catharsis through a careful mix of comedy and tears combined with an element of hope in the narrative. A great film must take the audience through peaks and valleys of emotion. For the most part, blockbusters are pure entertainment. Some of them attain an

MOTHER INDIA
Nargis with her sons Sunil
Dutt (holding machete) and
Rajendra Kumar. Dutt who
played a son to Nargis in the
film married her soon after
the completion of the film

PAKEEZAH

Meena Kumari in the
film, which depicts an
idealized portrayal of an
Indian courtesan and her
bid for respectability.

KAAGAZ KE PHOOL

Waheeda Rehman and
Guru Dutt in the first Indian
film made in cinemascope.

aura of respectability if, over time, they
continue to draw viewers. Classics make the
audience introspective about life. Their
innovative content or treatment may not
necessarily be commercially successful. *Do
Bigha Zamin* (1953) and *Devdas* (1955) earned
critical appreciation with low box-office
returns, but *Kaagaz Ke Phool* (1959) was an
absolute disaster, losing Rs.1.7 million, a huge
amount in the 1950s. Sometimes a classic only
gains recognition years after its initial release.

Elements of Novelty

Successful filmmakers often invent new ways
to portray old themes such as love. In *Padosan*
(1968), the hero's faked death prompts the
heroine to spontaneously express her feelings
for him. In *Maine Pyar Kiya*, a singing game
called *antakshari* becomes the vehicle through
which the heroine proclaims her love. In *Kuch
Kuch Hota Hai* (1998), an innocuous banter
between friends, Shah Rukh Khan and Kajol,
becomes an expression of affection.

DEVDAS

Dilip Kumar and Suchitra
Sen. In this film Dilip Kumar
developed his tragic hero
persona, portraying a man
experiencing unfulfilled
love and social taboos.

Blockbusters and classic films share a
literary quality. They foresee social issues,
and often frame them in the film text as the
tussle between tradition and modernity in
India. For example, *Andaz* (1949) explores
the impact of a capitalist economy on social
relationships. *Naya Daur* (1957) highlights
the problems of a rural economy in the age of
machines. Similarly, most Amitabh Bachchan
films capture the mood of the angry young
man disillusioned by the collapse of the
Nehruvian dream of an industrial India full
of job opportunities and financial security. In
the 1990s, a number of films dealt with the
cultural crisis faced by the Indian Diaspora
who survive in the West but feel a strong
attachment to India.

The 1930s and 1940s: Age of Reform and Experiment

With the advent of talkies in the 1930s, Hindi
films steadily moved from religious and
mythological subjects, to themes of contemporary social concern. As Gandhian ideals
gained currency, filmmakers discovered new
subjects revolving around the downtrodden
sections of Indian society.

Films such as *Achchut Kanya* (1936) and
Duniya Na Mane are deemed classics today
as they deal with issues that most people
preferred not to think about at the time of their
release. *Achchut Kanya*, directed by a
German, Franz Osten, highlights the sensitive
issue of caste in Hindu society. It portrays a
romance doomed to failure because the
protagonists belong to different social groups.
The film does not offer a radical solution, but
shows a love that knows no boundaries.
Duniya Na Mane tells of the quest of Nirmala
(Shanta Apte) forced to marry a man old
enough to be her father. In protest, she refuses
to allow her marriage to be consummated and
instead bonds with the widowed daughter of
her husband. The film's success prompted its
director, V. Shantaram, to take on other social
concerns, including Hindu-Muslim unity,

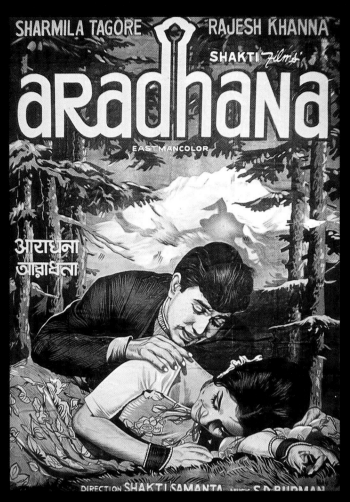

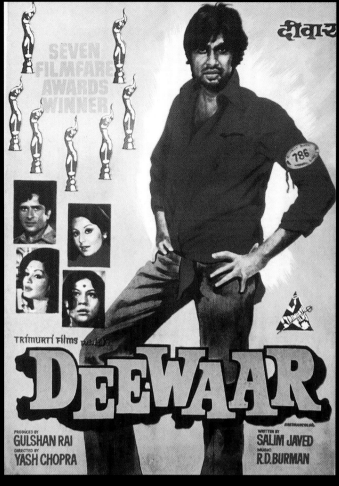

Posters depicting three of the biggest hits in the decades spanning 30 years of Bollywood; **NAYA DAUR** (1950s), **ARADHANA** (1960s) and **DEEWAR** (1970s)

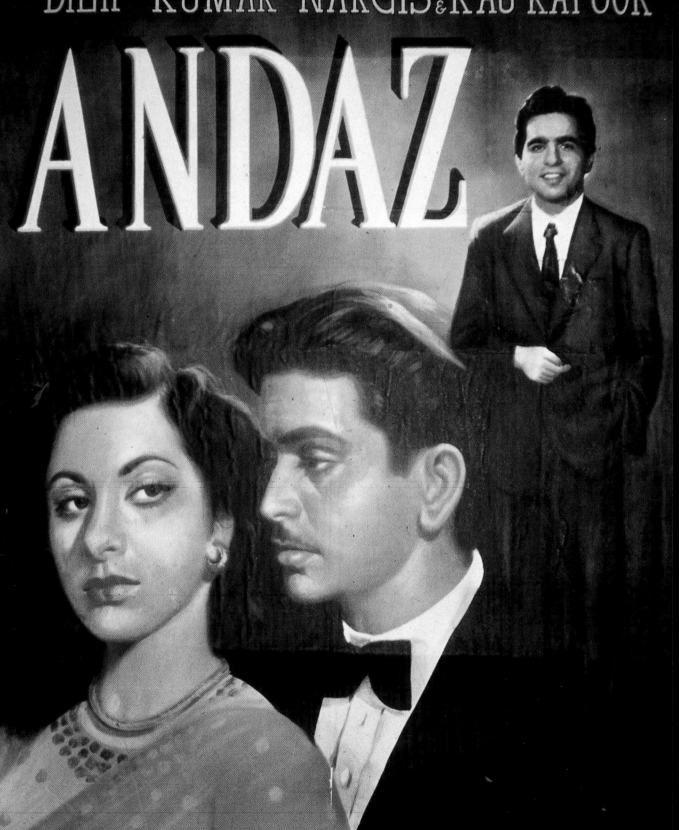

which he explores in *Padosi* (1941). Such films opened the way for the discussion of issues previously ignored at the popular level.

The licensing of film stock during the war years may have prompted a fresh look at content in Bollywood cinema. From this period came *Kismet*, the first ever blockbuster to run for as long as three years at a cinema hall in Calcutta. Though apparently inspired by Walter Wagner's *Algiers*, it marks the beginning of the narrative formula of long-lost brothers reunited, that future filmmakers would use tirelessly. *Kismet* created the image of a chain-smoking anti-hero who makes crime seem glamorous. The film's implicit anti-British stance, reflected in the song *Door Hato Ai Duniyawalo Hindustan Hamara Hai…* (Step back O outsiders! India belongs to us…), added to its huge popularity.

Political independence gained by India in 1947 fostered experimentation with cinematic form and content. *Kalpana* (1949), by the innovative dancer Uday Shankar, is one such effort. The film reflects an artist's vision of aesthetic unity through dance. A series of ballets suggest a common link between various Indian dance traditions. Though *Kalpana* was a miserable failure due to its weak narrative,

as a concept it remains unmatched. *Andaz*, ostensibly a love triangle, highlights a woman's vulnerable position in a society in transition where a woman can run an industry but can't have a man for a friend. She is provoked into killing a man, who mistakes her friendship for love, to show loyalty to her husband. *Andaz* has a modernistic feel. It is paced evenly with a number of hummable songs. The well-designed sets and the depth of shots heighten the beauty of the film's black-and-white photography. The racy dialogues are a far cry from the theatrical norm of the day. Its content and execution clearly make it a modern-day classic.

The 1950s and the 1960s: The Golden Years
Populist Social Realism

From the 1930s to the 1950s, films gradually evolved both in form and content and grew in sophistication. The dream sequence used for the first time in Raj Kapoor's film *Awara* (1951) became a symbol of hope for the common man in the new, independent India. Its song *Mujhko chahiye bahaar…* (I crave for Spring [Happiness]…) emphasizes the desires of ordinary people as represented by Raju (Raj Kapoor). In *Awara*, Raj Kapoor created

for himself the image of a Chaplinesque
vagabond trying to survive the city and its
harsh realities. Social environment, rather
than nature, is portrayed as wielding greater
influence on an individual's growth. This
theme struck a chord with the poor masses
everywhere. *Awara* became a big hit not only
in India but also in the former Soviet Union,
China and the Middle East.

Raj Kapoor's film *Shree 420* (1955) that
features the return of the Chaplinesque type of
character, contrasts the cloistered world of the
rich with the open spaces, or open heart, of
the poor. Kapoor's cinematic social realism,
best represented by the eventual triumph of
the underdog, endears him to the masses. His
films evoke a return to simplicity. In *Shree 420*,
Raj (Raj Kapoor) is torn between Vidya
(Nargis), loosely translated as knowledge,
and Maya (Nadira), meaning illusion, as he is
drawn into the vortex of crime. In the end,
however predictably, he realizes that honest
living is important. Raj Kapoor's films are
classics because they continue to entertain –
the dream world they create still satiates
viewers and critics alike. Beneath the
romantic gloss, Kapoor's films have class
conflict as a subtext. His team of writers

included a communist, Khwaja Ahmed Abbas.

B.R. Chopra's *Naya Daur* (1957) also
belongs to the populist tradition of social
realism. It dramatizes the basic conflict
between man and machine in a rural landscape. The dramatic tension in *Naya Daur*
centres on a race between a *tanga* (horse
carriage) and a bus. The prize in the race is
the monopoly of the village transport system.
Shankar (Dilip Kumar) the *tangawalla* is the
underdog, but he wins the race because he
drives along a new road made with collective
labour, a symbol of Gandhian bonhomie and
socialist camaraderie. His triumph marks a
victory for the people or a new dawn, as the
title of the film indicates. Elements of tension,
romance, comedy and the dreams of an ideal
village community in the narrative help
generate audience interest in the film.

The realist tradition within Bollywood

K.A. Abbas's film *Dharti Ke Lal* (1946), which
explored the Bengal famine of 1943, and De
Sica's *Bicycle Thieves* (1948), which was
shown at the First International Film Festival
at Bombay in 1952, may have prompted Bimal
Roy to dwell upon the Realist Tradition within
Bollywood school. Roy, like Raj Kapoor, tried to

NAYA DAUR

Dilip Kumar with his tanga.

DHARTI KE LAL

This film, set during World
War II, was the directorial
debut of Khwaja Ahmed
Abbas.

make cinema more meaningful. His *Do Bigha Zamin* underlines a peasant's struggle to reclaim his ancestral land. Shambhu (Balraj Sahni) is displaced from his village, thanks to a State-supported plan for industrialization. He and his son go to Calcutta (now Kolkata) in the hope of earning the money they need to retain their land. The father becomes a rickshaw-puller and the son a shoeshine boy. But harsh city life and bad luck force them to return to their village and the ultimate disillusionment of seeing an ugly factory standing on what was once Shambhu's farmland. *Do Bigha Zamin* reflects the realist-humanist contours of filmmaking within Bollywood, an evolution from the plain escapist screen romance to a critical review of rural India. Roy's treatment, marked by understatement and a fine perform-ance by Balraj Sahni, gives the film a great emotional depth and character. *Do Bigha Zamin* won an award at Cannes, and also received the National Certificate of Merit in 1953. When Raj Kapoor saw the film, he said he wished he could have made it – a tribute from one great filmmaker to another.

The 1950s also saw the return of the loser-hero, a novelty during the days of feel-good cinema. Based on Saratchandra

Chattopadhyay's novel, Bimal Roy's *Devdas* (1955) glorifies pain and unrequited love. It is the story of two childhood lovers forbidden to marry in caste-ridden Bengal. Roy's deftness in dealing with the rural milieu together with his languid style of cinematography inter-spersing narrative with shots of nature, gives *Devdas* its classic feel, despite its dismal performance at the box-office. The film shows *Devdas* (Dilip Kumar), wandering into the city after his beloved Paro (Suchitra Sen) marries someone else. He bumps into Chandramukhi (Vyjayanthimala), who develops a longing for him. But Devdas continues to live awkwardly straddled between the past and the present and dies on Paro's doorstep. Roy's visual motifs help align the narrative: during Devdas's aimless train trip – signifying a journey from nowhere to nowhere – a shot of the steam engine's belly-fire aptly reflects the heat and pain in his heart. The film offers multiple readings of the text. Two shades of femininity and love can be seen in the hero-ines: Paro is passionate, self-respecting and aggressive, and Chandramukhi is self-controlled and has a more giving nature. The film presents death as ultimate, transcending illusion and the reality of love. The confusion of

SHREE 420
Raj Kapoor. Here he plays a
vagabond that consolidated
his reputation. Kapoor's
character also had strong
shades of Charlie Chaplin.

PYAASA

Waheeda Rehman and

Guru Dutt.

PYAASA

Waheeda Rehman and
Guru Dutt.

opposite and below

MOTHER INDIA

This film acquired the

status of an Indian GONE

WITH THE WIND, was

seen as a national epic and

was a huge success.

illusion and reality is wonderfully depicted in a scene in which we see Chunni Babu (Moti Lal) trying to hang his walking stick on the shadow of a stand. He tries and fails, and throws away his stick. A close look into the emotional sensibilities of its characters gives *Devdas* a timeless feel.

Guru Dutt's films *Pyaasa* (1957) and *Kaagaz Ke Phool* look at man alienated from himself, society and nature. Both films are marked by great cinematography, in particular the use of silhouettes and beams of light in the tradition of Orson Welles's *Citizen Kane*. *Kaagaz Ke Phool* was the first film in India to be shot in cinemascope.

Pyaasa immortalizes a poet, Vijay (Guru Dutt), who gradually realizes the selfishness of the world of which he is a part. He rises above the biases of society. The usual norms of good and bad, love and hate become meaningless to him. *Pyaasa* was a commercial hit because its narrative mixes the comic with the serious, giving it an undulating feel that holds the interest of viewers. References in the film to the Hindu ideal of renunciation may have further endeared it to audiences.

Kaagaz Ke Phool deals with the theme of success and failure in life and love. It captures the moods of a man who suffers a dramatic reversal of fortune, finding himself an extra in the same film studio where he once ruled as a successful director. In true Bollywood tradition, fate plays an important part in the plot.

Both Roy and Dutt worked with established actors and achieved a certain musical feel in their films. They broke fresh ground by experimenting with narrative, sound, music and locale, and scripted a new visual odyssey without an overly burdensome concern for box-office success. Roy saw fame and fortune in his lifetime; Dutt's creative genius was truly appreciated only after his death.

Iconic Image

Mother India (1957) glorified woman as wife, as mother and as saviour of honour. Radha (Nargis) became the screen icon of the eternally suffering mother who is able to sacrifice her own son for the values she holds dear. That *dharma* (righteousness) must prevail over familial bonds is a perennially favourite theme of Bollywood filmmakers. In *Ganga Jamuna*, a brother kills his fugitive older brother for the sake of justice, and decades later in *Shakti* (1982), a father (Dilip Kumar) shoots his own son (Amitabh Bachchan) in

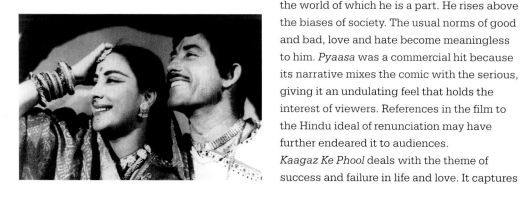

A poster of
MUGHAL-E-AZAM

MUGHAL-E-AZAM

Madhubala and Prithiviraj
Kapoor in K. Asif's Grand
Palace of Mirrors. In this
scene Anarkali incurs
Akbar's wrath with her
bold dance performance.

the name of the law.

Mother India is a remake of Mehboob
Khan's earlier film, *Aurat* (1940). It became a
success because of its empathetic treatment
of a woman and the sacrifice she makes with
allusions to the norm of ideal behaviour. It
plays on the emotions of love, jealousy, hatred
and honour in equal measure to tighten the
narrative for audiences. The film draws its
contemporary feel from the latent image of
change and development in rural India along
socialist lines. (Mehboob Khan's production
company used as its logo the Communist
symbol of a hammer and sickle).

Big Budget Extravaganza
The 1960s saw an expansion of big-budget
films. Setting the tone, director K.Asif's
Mughal-e-Azam (1960) narrates the tale of
mythological romance between Mughal
Emperor Akbar's son, Salim (Dilip Kumar),
and a palace maid Anarkali (Madhubala). The
film's romantic overtone has a subtext of
father-son discord, which remains a popular
narrative device in Bollywood cinema.
Prithviraj Kapoor's portrayal of Emperor Akbar
was, reputedly, a model of inspiration for
future actors. *Mughal-e-Azam* combines the

elements of a classic and a blockbuster, as
seen in its narrative drama, its grandeur of
scale and the sensuous appeal of ethereal
beauty Madhubala. It forms part of the
Bollywood's mythic lore – the grandeur of the
Mughal era recreated with expensive sets and
costumes, the dialogues in chaste Urdu, the
colour dance sequence shot in a specially
designed *sheesh-mahal* (Palace of Mirrors) set
– all still fascinate filmmakers and ordinary
viewers alike.

Waqt (1965) began the trend of multi-star
films. It brought together the combined
glamour of Sunil Dutt, Raj Kumar, Shashi
Kapoor, Sadhna and Sharmila Tagore. The film
was a smashing success. People still
remember verbatim the Raj Kumar dialogue
delivered with inimitable style: *Jani, yeh bach-
chon ke khelne ki cheez nahi…,* (Sweet Heart!
this (knife) is not a plaything for kids...) and
the wonderful foot-tapping Manna Dey song:
Ai meri zohra jabin. (O' my special one [full of
qualities]…). The theme of the film revolves
round the individual's struggle against his
fate. The lost-and-found formula is woven into
an interesting story of the ups and downs of a
family separated in an earthquake.

Another prominent film of the period was

Guide (1965). It touches upon questions of personal satisfaction, the imperfect nature of male-female relationships, and the Gandhian values of faith, simplicity and secularism. Its central character is a tour-guide turned saint, who sacrifices his life to uphold a traditional belief. The film's discourse reflects contemporary India, a young nation trying to come to terms with the forces of development and obscurantism. A symbolic argument about the linguistic superiority of English over Sanskrit parallels serious dilemmas faced by the lead characters in the story and reflects the underlying conflict between desire and fulfillment.

The film is excellently framed and the camera movements add to the power of the narrative. One feels the exhilaration as Waheeda Rehman ecstatically dances to the song, *Aaj phir jeene ki tamanna hai…*(Today I again desire to live…). Director Vijay Anand, like Bimal Roy, ensures that the songs in his film merge meaningfully with the narrative and, like Roy, he does not state the obvious. The song sequences in *Guide* have a natural dream-like quality.

In his film *Teesri Manzil* (1966), Vijay Anand changed gears by making a musical murder mystery in which an Elvis Presley-like character, Rocky (Shammi Kapoor), is mistaken for the murderer of a young girl. Rocky is able to prove his innocence after several contortions of the plot, but the taut screenplay builds suspense until the bitter end. *Teesri Manzil* established R.D. Burman as the music director of the new generation with songs such as *Aaja aaja main hun pyar tera* (Come, come to me for I'm your love…) and *O mere sona re, sona re sona re* (O' my lover boy…).

Literary Gems

A number of films in the 1960s drew upon the gems of Indian literature directly or indirectly. Critically acclaimed *Sahib Bibi aur Ghulam* (1962, Abrar Alvi) is based on a Bengali novel by Bimal Mitra and captures with finesse the gradual decline of the Bengali feudal aristocracy in the early twentieth century. The film's ambience, narration and flow depict the quirky world of the *zamindars* (or landed aristocracy). It also evokes images of love and hate as it portrays the desire of Choti Bahu (Meena Kumari) for her husband, a desire that makes her ready to sacrifice even her reputation and her life. The woman's strong character is laudable, but perhaps her craving for sexual fulfillment failed to appeal

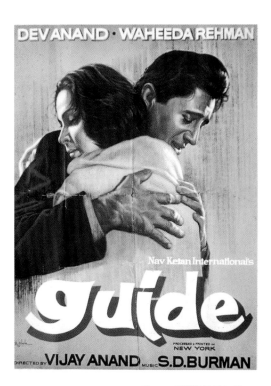

SAHIB BIBI AUR GHULAM
Guru Dutt and Meena Kumari
in Abrar Alvi's classic film
about the Bengali aristocracy in
the early 20th century.

TEESRI KASAM
Raj Kapoor and Waheeda
Rehman; The story was
based on the platonic love
between a bullock cart
driver and a stage actress.

to the public. Consequently, despite its balanced screenplay, fine performances and great songs, the film managed only an average collection at the box-office. *Sahib Bibi aur Ghulam* was rated highly for its creative treatment and for its realistic feel. It bears the unmistakable stamp of Guru Dutt, though it was his close associate, Abrar Alvi, who directed the film.

Another film with a strong literary flavour is *Teesri Kasam* (1966). Based on Phaniswar Nath Renu's story, *Mare Gaye Gulfam*, the film is a subtle evocation of the platonic love between Hiraman, a bullock-cart driver (Raj Kapoor) and a rural stage actress Hirabai (Waheeda Rehman). Raj Kapoor, having developed perfect mannerisms for his role, speaks and reacts verbally in a way that 'iss' unforgettable. Visual images and dialogues, aided by songs such as *Pan khaye saiyan hamaro* (My lover [can be singled out for] he chews betel leaves…) and *Duniya banane wale* (O, Creator of the world…) bring alive the magic of rural existence. In spite of its indisputable aesthetic value, the film failed commercially.

Ganga Jamuna was written, produced, and some say ghost-directed by Dilip Kumar.

Set in a north Indian rural landscape, it presents the lives of two brothers who love each other, but, as victims of circumstance, end up on opposite sides of the law. Ultimately, the younger brother Jamuna (Nasir Khan) shoots the outlaw elder brother Ganga (Dilip Kumar) to uphold justice, a dramatic twist later copied in *Deewaar* (1975).

Visually, *Ganga Jamuna* is more direct than the films of Bimal Roy set in a rural milieu. However, in its treatment, it draws much from Roy's works: Kamla's (Azra) nocturnal visit to Jamuna's house to profess her love is reminiscent of Paro's similar effort in *Devdas*; Anwar Hussain as the village landlord is modelled on the character of Ugra Narayan (Pran) of *Madhumati*.

Ganga Jamuna is a classic blockbuster. It blends believable characters, hit music and excellent camerawork to form a landmark film in the history of Bollywood cinema. A train robbery scene from the film stands for its superb execution, where bandits astride horses are shown through the moving wheels of a train. This shot was imitated, as brilliantly, almost fifteen years later in *Sholay* (1975), another Bollywood blockbuster.

NAYA DAUR

Dilip Kumar and
Vyjayanthimala.

Opposite page
MADHUMATI

Dilip Kumar and
Vyjayantimala in
a film that dealt with
murder, romance and
rebirth.

Posters of **PADOSAN** and
CHALTI KA NAM GADI

Solid Entertainers

Madhumati (1958) was a smash hit of the late
1950s. It introduced the concept of eternal
love, of lovers uniting in life after death,
drawing from the Hindu belief in rebirth, and
facilitating viewer-identification with the
narrative. *Madhumati* recounts the story of a
dead woman who helps her beloved avenge
her murder. The suspense in the plot remains
latent till the end: the apparent use of the
cinematic device of a double-role works as a
ploy to keep the audience guessing. The film's
popularity rests on a great story that is a
delight to watch.

Chalti Ka Nam Gadi (1958) fine-tuned the
comic genre in Bollywood, blending funny
situations and a racy plot. The film's appeal
lies in the almost fantasy-like romance
between a beautiful city girl (Madhubala) and
a car mechanic (Kishore Kumar). The subplot,
involving eccentric brothers and an element of
mystery, lends drama to the film.

Its songs are still popular and the famous
Ik ladki bhigi bhagi si (A drenched roving
damsel…) number was recently re-mixed in
a pop album. *Chalti Ka Nam Gadi* proved that
the maverick actor-producer Kishore Kumar
could sing, act funny and command respect –

a rare combination in a comedian.

Padosan (1968) is another film in the genre
of fun and frivolity. Its simple romantic story
derives strength from master performances
by Kishore Kumar as a dramatist-musician,
Mehmood as a south Indian music and dance
teacher who speaks Hindi with a funny
accent, and Sunil Dutt as Bhola, who couldn't
have looked more stupid, or innocent as his
name implies. *Padosan* was a hit because of
its songs and its original comic situations,
including a musical duel between two singers.

The 1970s and 1980s: The Age of Transition

The 1970s saw the rise of mega-budget Hindi
cinema with a semi-urban or urban backdrop.
Films began to reflect issues closer to the vast
mass of people who had moved from rural
areas to big towns. At the same time, 'middle-
of-the-road' cinema – films by Hrishikesh
Mukherjee, Basu Chatterji and Gulzar – found
firm roots among city-bred audiences.

Middle-of-the-road-Cinema

Middle-of-the-road cinema portrayed the
guy-next-door in real-life situations. It had
a certain freshness and was devoid of
customary violence. Good music continued

CHALTI KA NAM GADI
Madhubala and Kishore
Kumar in a film that tells the
story of a sensuous city girl
who meets a naive, bumbling
car mechanic.

to be a part of its universe. *Anand* (1970) starring the reigning superstar, Rajesh Khanna and Amitabh, the superstar-to-be, is perhaps one of the best examples of middle-of-the-road cinema that was widely seen and appreciated. The film unravels the joyous and inspiring story of a man dying of liver cancer, propagating a positive outlook on life and a strong belief in humanity.

Aandhi (1975) is a tale of a chance coming-together of an estranged married couple after years of separation. They share moments of warmth and nostalgia and then move away as quietly as they had met. The film is refreshing, enchanting and believable to city audiences. Melodious songs help to connect the viewer with the on-screen romantic celebration of private moments. Images from *Aandhi* seem to induce a feeling of serenity that even repeated viewing of the film fails to dissipate. Director Gulzar's poetic touches in the *mise-en-scène* – long stretches of silence with natural sound in the background in the tradition of Bimal Roy – make *Aandhi* a pleasure to watch. The film was only a moderate success and was even banned temporarily because of perceived similarities between the film's female lead and the then Prime Minister of India, Indira

Gandhi. Yet, the film's artistic merit has not faded with the times, and hence it qualifies to be rated a classic.

Gulzar's *Ijaazat* (1987) recreates the tingling sensation of a mature romance. It looks at an unusual male-female relationship, a subject less often broached in Hindi films. Rekha and Naseeruddin Shah give us a glimpse of the pain, anguish, jealousy and happiness of a couple who meet unexpectedly at a deserted railway station after years spent apart. Their brief encounter brings back a flood of memories and poses the silent question: what went wrong in their relationship? The film exudes a sentimental feeling that seems more touching than the recent teenybopper romance stories. Gulzar's symbolic imagery is translated into song by R.D. Burman.

All-time Favourites: Classic Blockbusters
Sholay (1975), an enormously successful film that ran continuously for five years at a cinema hall in Mumbai, was a mixture of Sergio Leone's spaghetti Westerns and Akira Kurosawa's *Seven Samurai* (1954). Beautifully photographed by Dwarka Divecha, the film portrays a man seeking to avenge the murder

of his family, with help from two small-time criminals.

The film has action, comedy and tragedy – all in the right amounts and at the right intervals. In the opening scene a police inspector (Sanjeev Kumar) and two kind-hearted hoodlums (Amitabh and Dharmendra) fight bandits on a train. A little later a comic jailer (Asrani) directs his officials to keep an eye on the prisoners, but tragedy strikes when the inspector loses his family to the bandit leader Gabbar (Amjad Khan). A similar chain of events is subtly repeated throughout the film.

This film about revenge created an iconic villain in Gabbar Singh, the role that was offered to several actors before Amjad Khan. Gabbar's mean smile and ferocious demeanour seem to reflect the rural bandit in real life.

Sholay failed to do well initially, but box-office sales improved dramatically after the release of the soundtrack including Salim-Javed's lusty dialogues, *Arre, O Sambha…* (Hey Sambha …[Gabbar addresses his trusted lieutenant]); *Kitne aadmi the …* (How many men did you face? …). The Salim-Javed duo had earlier helped put Amitabh Bachchan on the road to stardom with the characterization

of the angry young man in *Zanjeer* (1973). Amitabh Bachchan, quiet and brooding, fits the image perfectly. *Zanjeer*'s anti-hero is forced to battle his parents' killer in order to rid himself of nightmares – a novel element in the script. The huge commercial success of the film proved that audiences could like a hero who broke the law, provided it was for a personal cause.

Deewaar (1975), another of Salim-Javed's creations, rehashes the old formula of sibling rivalry and imbues the image of the angry young man with a pan-Indian, secular face. Its taut screenplay highlights a dockworker's meteoric rise through crime and the emotional conflict his success brings. The drama and tension in the sibling relationship may have been inspired by the Hollywood film *Public Enemy* (1931), in which the irrepressible James Cagney repeatedly gets into arguments with his elder brother about his notorious reputation and ill-gotten wealth.

Deewaar is an example of truly excellent characterization with an immaculately controlled performance by Amitabh that gives his gangster persona a human face and makes the audience root for him. It is a modern day classic that has universal appeal even

SHOLAY

Dharmendra and Amitabh Bachchan, in one of the greatest Bollywood blockbusters. Amitabh then went on to become a one-man industry who ruled Bollywood until the early 1990s.

twenty-five years after it was made.

Amar Akbar Anthony, (1977), another film based on the 'lost-and-found' formula, is thoroughly entertaining. A pure 'masala', it is sprinkled with many stars and a surfeit of action, emotion, drama, comedy and tragedy built around a tale of separation within a family. Three lost brothers are each raised by people belonging to different faiths – Hindu, Muslim and Christian (a moral for national unity). They continue to meet accidentally without realizing they are related. The end is predictable: the happy union of the family. The film has many memorable scenes, such as that of the drunk Anthony (Amitabh) applying some salve onto his mirror-image after being hit. Amitabh's drunken dialogue in 'Bombaiyya Hindi' (Bombay street Hindi) was an absolute hit, and later directors in film after film would insist on Amitabh providing comic relief with a similar kind of act. The film's success was partly due to Laxmikant Pyarelal's musical score and popular songs such as: *My name is Anthony Gonsalves* and *Anhonee ko honi kar de* ([We can] make the impossible happen…).

Period Romance

Pakeezah (1972) lends dignity to a courtesan drama. It takes a closer look at the life of one woman and her struggle to achieve respectability. Kamal Amrohi, a master of historical drama, evokes a glamorized but pain-filled image of a marginalized Muslim dancer catering to the feudal elite. The narrative, the beautiful sets and Ghulam Mohammad's music help build the myth of a courtesan with a heart of gold. Amrohi uses a train as a recurring motif to symbolize the internal desire of Sahibjaan (Meena Kumari) to break free from her cloistered existence. The film had a weak opening, but it picked up following Meena Kumari's death, a month after the release.

Muzaffar Ali's *Umrao Jaan* (1981) reflects the new aesthetics that developed as a result of the rise of a genre of cinema that grew alongside or parallel to Bollywood films. Based on an Urdu novel by Mirza Mohammad Hadi Ruswa, *Umrao Jaan* plays on the popular theme of the isolation and pain hidden under the outward grandeur of a courtesan who is at once an object of lust, awe and pity.

Rekha, as Umrao, lends an added dimension to the screenplay, which depicts the

decline and disintegration of a sophisticated cultural milieu, as British rule in India expands and becomes consolidated. *Umrao Jaan* is a complete cinematic experience for film buffs. Excellent imagery, poetry, ghazals and soulful music envelop Umrao's tender emotions in a bundle of exquisite beauty and rhythm. It was a rare commercial and artistic success.

Celebrating Teenage Love

Seeking legitimacy for love unfettered by considerations of class or religion, Raj Kapoor's *Bobby* launched a thousand emotions. The freshness of the lead actors, Dimple Kapadia and Rishi Kapoor, made teenage rebellion fashionable and breathed new life into the clichéd plot. The charming innocence of their faces caught the public fancy, and people saw the film over and over again. The frenzied mania may be absent today but Raj Kapoor's visually original and brilliant evocation of the special chemistry of first love, endures. The image of Dimple, with her hair partly smeared in flour when she sees Rishi for the first time, was drawn from a real life incident between Raj Kapoor and Nargis. Kapoor maintained if a filmmaker is sure about what he says, people always respond positively. *Bobby* is still liked by the masses because it seems so genuine.

Sooraj Barjatya's *Maine Pyar Kiya* was the biggest grosser of 1989. It was surprising that a first-time director using absolutely unknown actors could produce such a good film but, like Raj Kapoor, Barjatya was sure of his ideas. He took a love story and worked it around the values he thought audiences would relate to. The narrative combines the traditional Indian values of respect and personal warmth with the western values of individuality and the dignity of labour. *Maine Pyar Kiya* became a massive hit because it straddled the poles of glamour and simplicity and sent the message that wealth is fine, but warmth and respect for human relationships is a virtue. This enabled the film to communicate with a newer generation of film-goers.

The Frilly 1990s and the New Millennium

The 1990s saw increasing technical sophistication in the quality of films made in Bollywood. Filmmakers became concerned with the look and feel of films. They began to scout picturesque locations abroad and started to use soft-focus photography to give a dreamy quality to the visuals. This worked

BOBBY

Rishi Kapoor and Dimple
Kapadia.

SHREE 420

Raj Kapoor and Nargis.
The celebrity couple of
Bollywood in the 1950s.

well with new romance stories involving NRIs.

Love redefined

Lamhe (1991) elevates love to a higher plane.
Director Yash Chopra, a self-confessed
romanticist, blurs the lines defining modern
and traditional mores by portraying the love
of a girl for her dead mother's suitor. *Lamhe*
celebrates love as having dual forms, which
can either induce submission to the beloved
or offer the power to guide. The original
content, despite having the usual Bollywood
trappings of songs, dances, comedy etc., was
perhaps a little ahead of its time. Chopra was
accused of breaking a taboo, but was also
praised for his tale of inter-generational
romance. The film achieved considerable
critical acclaim, but hardly the commercial
success it deserved.

Return to Family and Roots

Hum Apke Hain Kaun (1994), though
dismissed in a pre-release assessment as a
wedding home video, ended up earning an
estimated profit of $ 20.8 million. The film's
drama is rooted in the development and
growth of family relationships. Its 14 songs are
meant to replace the spoken word and carry

the narrative forward. Following Bollywood
tradition, circumstance or fate acts as the
villain in *Hum Apke Hain Kaun*. According to
the director Sooraj Barjatya, the success of the
film was rooted in its small town feel, its typically Indian flavour, particularly its upholding
family values, traditions and sacrifice.

Dilwale Dulhaniya Le Jayenge (1995) gives
the NRI a new respectability. The film is about
a romance that starts in the UK and ends in
India. There are problems and crises in the
relationship, yet the NRI Shah Rukh Khan
does not give up and, unlike the hero in *Bobby*,
waits until the girl's father relents. The
feel-good narrative, overt sentimentality and
the appeal of the young stars Kajol and Shah
Rukh Khan, made the film a success.

Kuch Kuch Hota Hai (1998) accords legitimacy to a second marriage, a phenomenon
that has only recently gained respectability
among the Indian middle classes. Despite
a certain 'Archie Comics' feel, the film
introduces a novel element into the romantic
narrative: a daughter pushes her father to seek
love again. The film explores the wafer-thin
divide between friendship and love, and
shows how two women can bond despite
loving the same man. Its commercial success

**DILWALE DULHANIYA LE
JAYENGE**

Shah Rukh Khan and Kajol.
A NRI love story filmed
abroad.

flows from its thematic combination of the western mind set and the Indian heart as epitomized in a previous film song from *Awaara*, *Mera Joota hai Japani, Ye patloon Inglistani, Sar pe lal topi Russi, Phir bhi dil hai Hindustani,* (My shoes are Japanese, my pants are English, [my] head wears a Russian hat, yet my heart remains Indian).

Ugly Urban Saga

Away from the wishy-washy lifestyle of *Kuch Kuch Hota Hai* stands *Satya* (1999), a grim tale of urban violence. It reflects the uncertainty of contemporary times that pushes an innocent youngster Satya (Chakravarthy) to crime, and which soon sucks him deeper into its vortex. He meets a tragic end, dying at the door of the girl he loves (Urmila Matondkar). The film became a hit because for the first time, perhaps, reel villains were shown as real people. Bhiku Mhatre (Manoj Bajpai), like Gabbar in *Sholay*, is an iconic character. He

is a dreaded gangster, but generally lets his wife dominate the household. He lives in an ordinary home and banters with both his family and his associates in crime. He is hot-headed, but less complicated than many people. *Satya* is chilling and horrifying yet a treat to watch again and again due to its honest treatment of its subject.

Film of the Millennium

Kaho Naa Pyaar Hai was the film of 2000. It symbolizes the hopes and aspirations of the current generation just as *Bobby* and *Maine Pyar Kiya* had done earlier. Through packaging unknown faces in a familiar script, portraying a dash of crime, an exotic locale and fancy dance routines, *Kaho Naa Pyaar Hai* provides unalloyed entertainment to the audience. The allusions to true love and justice in the screenplay add the necessary drama. The film exudes visible style in the framing of shots and the mise-en-scène. It became a hit on account of its glamorous sheen, and a thoroughly natural performance in front of the camera by the talented, good-looking new star Hrithik Roshan.

Epilogue

Despite the homogenous look of the 1990s and an apparent absence of substance and style, Bollywood continues to inspire all kinds of film professionals whose work has a therapeutic value and everlasting appeal to mass audiences. In addition to box-office successes, these films are tirelessly aired on cable TV. The typical world of Bollywood cinema with its perfect mix of myth and reality, creates both the dream and the joy of its fulfillment.

KAHO NA PYAAR HAI
Hrithik Roshan, new heart throb of the young generation.

Heart of the Movie

The Hindi film… Is it the path to collective *Nirvana*? Or the Viagra that promises ecstasy? In the broadest sense, mainstream cinema meets the emotional and cultural needs of a people who may be divided by language and ethnicity, but are united in their addiction to the multifarious joys of the Hindi film. It is the overflowing *thali* that tickles the taste buds and takes the consumer to a paradise of satiety – though this is not so much a gourmet's delight, as the basic satiation of a glutton's indiscriminating hunger for entertainment.

The Hindi film's seduction of our senses is also overlaid with an uplifting morality – an urgent need to ennoble. This contradiction reflects the teeming existential conflicts of India itself. As the most potent and most persuasive form of mass entertainment, film contains all the influences that have been shaping the Indian sensibility.

The ancient Indian *Navrasa* theory (the nine states of emotion), which classifies aesthetic enjoyment, does not apply only to the classical arts. Indians who may not have heard of the *Natya Shastra* (Science of Dramatology by Bharat Muni) are instinctively *rasikas* (or connoisseurs) when it comes to films. Our interest in a work – of drama or epic discourse – centres on 'certain primary sentiments felt by all human beings … love, heroism, and pathos'. The rhetorical expression of these sentiments seems to satisfy a deep, instinctive craving. This is because the stories and characters are always variations of the same stereotype, the unfolding is predetermined, the *dénouement* predictable. And our audiences lap up the comforting joys of predictability. *Rasa*, the enjoyment of a particular flavour, has percolated down into the popular art forms, so that the Hindi film is able to accommodate the sentimentality of traditional drama and the robustness of folk forms such as *Nautanki*.

The very art of Bollywood story-telling possesses an astonishing degree of elasticity. A traditional narrator, unfolding stirring epic battles or exemplary tales of devotees, will stray from his narrative to swipe an irreverent paw at the political establishment or a local bigwig, confident that his audience will follow his departures from the known story. Performers like the wandering *Kathakars* (story-tellers) and exponents of *Harikatha* (narrators of religious lore) lace their discourse

MISSION KASHMIR

Hrithik Roshan plays an angst-ridden terrorist who can also dance.

below

BAIJU BAWRA

Meena Kumari and Bharat Bhushan elevate love to the highest level.

Govinda and Aishwarya Rai

with songs and impromptu dances. Alienation and stylization are older than borrowed Brechtian techniques. An academically inclined defender of Hindi cinema's song-and-dance routine has only to look at the living Indian tradition. As for ordinary viewers, theories can wait while they hum the latest Rahman or Anu Malik number and indulge

their travelogue fantasy while they watch the Karismas and Hrithiks of Bollywood dance in Switzerland or Scotland or even the Antipodes.

Rasa is the *raison d'être* of music. In India, this most sublime of arts manages to reconcile two apparent irreconcilables – a rigid structure and free improvization. In classical music, a *raga* has an inviolable structure, a set scale of ascending and descending notes: the musician's artistry lies precisely in being able to deftly improvize phrases, gliding over the notes while changing the stress with wonderful subtlety. Even in the less exalted realm of *ghazals* (Urdu love poetry) and *geets* (Hindi lyrical poetry), it is the subtle shift and particular emphasis on a word, a note or the entire phrase, that sends listeners into a frenzy of appreciative *Wah Wahs*! The story of the Hindi film is set within this rigid structure. What the audience eagerly looks for is improvization within the formula. So, we experience the pleasures of recognition – of conventions and departures from them – without having to invent genres such as Hollywood. One can say that the Hindi movie is a super-genre that combines within itself all the genres.

HIMMAT
Sunny Deol and Tabu. A
scene typical of the make-
believe world of Bollywood.

Posters of **JAGTE RAHO**,
BAIJU BAWARA, **AAG**
and **PYAASA**.
All films were significant
successes during the
Golden Era.

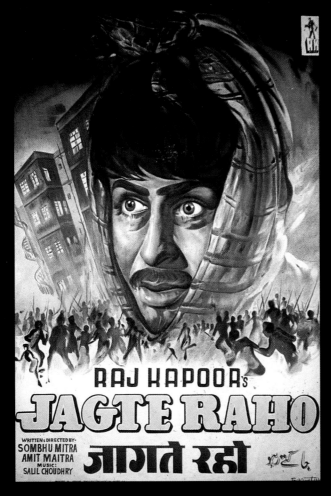

This all-in-one genre is testament to the Indian ability to take a commercial art form born in the West and make it wholly Indian – in spirit at least. Call it happenstance or fate in the land of Karma. The predictable coincidences proliferating in our formulaic films buffer us against the uncertainties of life. They act as a kind of a safety valve for an ancient civilization hurtled into modernity and nation-statehood without the benefit of an evolutionary historical process.

That, at least, is one way of explaining the monotonously familiar Hindi *filmi* formula, where virtue and tradition triumph over vice and modernity (the two being almost synonymous), and the glamorous star cast, performing rather than acting, is all set to woo, tease, titillate as well as uplift the audience. The Hindi film is a simple morality play or tale of modern times. In a land of unequal opportunity and rigid hierarchies, of vast disparities stoically borne, where for centuries life was at the mercy of capricious elements, the certitudes of comforting myths and escapist fantasies are just as essential as air and water. Ambiguity is anathema and simple morality must prevail. This is the Indian version of the feel-good factor that Hollywood

producers arrive at after testing audience response.

The feel-good factor has to be more than simply the triumph of good over evil. The evil has to look larger than life, to mimic the archetypal proportions of a Ravana against whom Rama will wage a righteous war. In India, mythology is part and parcel of current idiomatic speech. Characters and incidents from the *Ramayana* and *Mahabharata* are ready reckoners for a host of situations and emotions and value-systems. The matrix of metaphors is indeed rich beyond imaging, whether in a trite self-conscious thriller or in a work of the 'new cinema'. *Vaastav* (1999) and *Ardh Satya* (1983), for instance, are two films from near opposite ends of the artistic spectrum that use the epic metaphor of a hero caught in a *chakravyuha* (no-exit trap), amplified to the contemporary context.

And so villains have grown exaggeratedly colourful, even *outré* – Amrish Puri's graph of evil deeds soars into the stratosphere of unreality – because the hero must slay a most incredibly horrid monster to justify his heroism. The hero has no intimate enemies and personal demons but has to invoke Rama's exalted sense of duty, or Krishna's

MOHRA

Mohra means a pawn. The film is a slick thriller in whcih Naseeruddin Shah (centre) is the master who pits one pawn(Sunil Shetty) against the other (Akshay Kumar)

Preity Zinta, the vivacious star
who was first spotted by director
Shekhar Kapur.

opposite page
Govinda and Raveena Tandon in
AUNTY NO 1.

erotic playfulness and wisdom, or Arjun's
paralyzed will at the critical moment of action,
or the rash valour of Abhimanyu caught in a
maze from which there is no escape. Other
characters are similarly drawn from the epics.
The patient, chaste and suffering wife must be
Sita, the intrepid doer of brave deeds is Durga,
the doting foster mother who has to give up
her own son is Yashoda, the lovelorn rustic
belle is Radha… and so it goes on, never
missing a mythic beat. And of course, the
Hindi screen goddess is a seductive *apsara*
come down to earth. Just think of Madhuri and
her heaving, chartbusting *Dhak Dhak dhadke
jiya* (My heart beats loudly…) from *Beta* (1992).
She is the modern Menaka – ascetic ochre
never looked more seductive – drawing the
shy hero away from his self-imposed vow of
chastity. The *apsara* look – bare midriff,
clinging chiffon tightly draped around a body
encased in glittering jewellery – is mandatory
for at least part of a song, even if the heroine
then slips into a swirling mini or flowing
lehanga. The dress designer manufactures
dreams for all the viewers. While panting
males get their fix of sexual fantasy, adoles-
cent girls and young women mentally jot
down fashion notes. The Hindi film is mapping

MUGHAL-E-AZAM
Madhubala immortalizes
Anarkali, the lovely court
dancer who defies the
might of the Mughal
emperor, all for the love of
the Crown Prince.

out a brand new mythology of female sexuality
on celluloid before our very eyes. Remember,
it is the filmic Viagra for our sexually frenetic
times.

Mythology has been called the shorthand
of a people's history. Hindi films are notori-
ously ahistorical – anachronisms abound
happily, with no trace of embarrassment.
In a country where everything ancient is
consigned to some vague Vedic age, where
record-keeping is an extremely inventive
exercise, with lots of input from a freely

UMRAO JAAN
Rekha as the exquisitely
cultivated courtesan who
enthralls half of nineteenth-
century Lucknow.

During the 1970s and 1980s
Amitabh Bachchan often
played an angry young man.

opposite page
EK RISHTAA
The grand patriarch Amitabh
Bachchan embraces his son
Akshay Kumar – the family
always triumphs

roaming imagination, why should there be
a fuss about historical accuracy? What need
is there for documentation backed by
painstaking research? We, as a people, are
careless with and about our history, so we get
the historicals we deserve. Thus, the Sohrab
Modi spectaculars, *Sikandar* (1941) and *Pukar*
(1939), which transport Parsi theatre onto the
screen, seem realistic enough. But history, in
the sense of drawing the emotional graph of a
people, is very much alive and kicking in the
Hindi film. The urgent need to say everything
in a heightened manner, the amazingly casual
yet loaded references to epic heroes and gods,
the zeal to raise the outcome to an acceptable
moral level – these are what keep the heart
of the Hindi film beating with such healthy
regularity.

Hindi cinema's first method actor – Dilip
Kumar – mined the vein of inexplicable
melancholy with superb artistry in a host of
dark-hued films like *Shikast* (1953), *Footpath*
(1953), *Jogan* (1950) and *Mela* (1948). However,
melancholy and tragic introspection hardly
feature in Hindi films. The script of the Hindi
film does not believe in modern-day
psychobabble. The first concern is to radiate
warm reassurance and a sunny optimism.

Though the individual may brood and give in
to bouts of despair, the immediate family, and
the larger family that is the nation, must
continue to uphold the old values of filial piety,
submission to divine justice and doing one's
dharma (or duty). It is like reverting to the
equilibrium of the *status quo,* after a brief

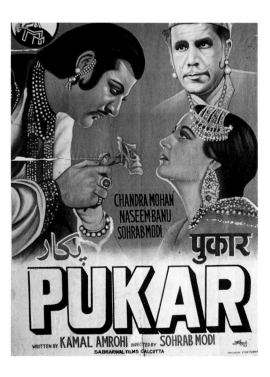

pause for individual sorrow. In *Deewaar* (1975), a truly modern tragedy, Vijay's doomed life is recalled by his mother, in whose arms he dies. Similarly, in *Shakti* (1982), a film of unmatched poignancy, Amitabh dies in the arms of his father, an honest policeman who places duty above a father's love. Those who are at the centre of the code of *dharma* live on to tell the sad tale. The death of the errant hero is an exception to the rule where the family must reclaim its lost son.

The Hindi film is thus more than an escapist dream. We often tend to overlook the obvious truth – popular cinema, catering to a mass audience, has the uncanny ability to absorb and reflect the *zeitgeist,* both directly and obliquely. The Hindi film relates the continuum of ancient conflicts, eternal dilemmas and everyday problems; it captures the astonishing coexistence of sublime art and calendar *kitsch,* of intellectual sophistication and *bazaar* garishness. Out of this bewildering excess, the audience chooses what it wants and discards the redundant parallel stories, the tacked-on comedy track and the predictable ending.

It is amusing how many Indians saw *Titanic* (which was stupendously successful in India) as a typically mushy Hindi film on a lavish scale. But this equation overlooked one essential difference: the unhappy ending, which is prohibited in the Sanskrit drama tradition of the *Natya Sastra*. This hoary dictat still seems to prevail in the more popular legends of star-crossed lovers. In a country where horoscopes are religiously matched after the caste equations are sorted out to general satisfaction, where dowries are haggled over by bargaining experts, where *muhurats* (auspicious moments) are picked out by pundits with the precision required for a rocket launch, viewers want at least the screen lovers to enjoy the happiness of eternal togetherness. For every errant *Qayamat Se Qayamat Tak* (1988) – our equivalent of Romeo and Juliet in Thakurland – there are hundreds of aspiring *Maine Pyar Kiya* (1989) clones who surmount the rich–poor divide.

Hindi cinema is to India what Hollywood is to the world. The world's largest and perhaps most chaotic democracy has joined the world's most powerful democracy in creating and exporting its mass media. The Movie Moghuls of Mumbai now aspire to reach markets beyond the enclaves of well-heeled nostalgic Non-Resident Indians (NRIs). They

Shah Rukh Khan and Juhi
Chawla in a scene reflective
of the growing permissive-
ness in Bollywood.

CHAL MERE BHAI
Karisma Kapoor with Salman
Khan and Sanjay Dutt, who
play inseparable brothers.

have stopped being apologetic about the
masala they add with calculated cunning to
the brew of heady entertainment. Of course,
the Bombay film does not have the reach or
sheer scale of the Hollywood product, but its
makers are quick learners. The savvy vendors
of the Indian-made dream know the USP of
their product – high melodrama, soul-haunting
melodies, songs that unleash pelvic-thrusting
gyrations, dances that veil the get-me-now
sexuality of the music video with the exotic
allure of eastern seduction.

Essentially, the Hindi film is all heart – and
no brain, say its critics, confounded and even
outraged by its enduring popularity. This
popularity is not confined to India. It spills
over into pockets of the world where the
Indian Diaspora has settled and even reaches
places where Hindi is an alien tongue. In
Nepal, Bangladesh, the Middle East, many

parts of Africa, Malaysia, Indonesia, Australia
and the erstwhile Soviet Union, Hindi films
amuse and entertain, enchant and enthrall or
even annoy, but are not ignored. Whether they
are competently dubbed, subtitled, or entirely
untranslated, does not really seem to matter.
The basic strengths of colour, emotion, family
values, music and dance manage to overcome
any linguistic barrier. People in Egypt recog-
nize Amitabh Bachchan instantly though they
may struggle to put a name to the face of the
Indian Prime Minister. Likewise, *Awara hoon*
was warbled in the former Soviet Union, and
Raj Kapoor was practically an honorary Soviet
citizen. For a people served up boy-meets-
tractor tales of Socialist Realism, Kapoor's
persona of a carefree tramp, happy with his
lot, was a merry slap at authoritarianism –
though of course no one saw it that way at
the time.

HUM JAWAB DENGE

Sridevi in a typical wet

sari sequence.

Madhuri Dixit immortalized
by Gautam Rajadhyaksha,
in his studio.

As for the yearning NRIs all over the globe, the Hindi film is the umbilical cord that anchors them to their past, to Indian culture and its norms. One might think the second and third generation of NRI kids – often dubbed Abcds (American born confused *desis)* in the US – would have moved away from the staple fare of their parents, since they have grown up with Hollywood and MTV, but their fractured psyche seems to hang on with even greater passion to the easiest form of bonding with the mother country. Public-access television in the US shows locally made programmes featuring the doings of the NRI community – clips of an obligatory *Bharata Natyam* (a form of South Indian classical dance) or a music concert, discussions with a visiting Indian VIP – rounded off with the mandatory songs from Hindi films. Be prepared, unsuspecting visitor to the US! A slot called *Shadi Ka Hungama* (Marriage Furore) telecasts wedding videos invariably starring nubile *desi* girls who twirl, whirl, pout and pirouette to the latest hot numbers from Mumbai, amidst the indulgent *desi* and amazed western guests. One week it could be a desperate Aishwarya wannabe prancing to the *Nimbuda* number, while the next it could be a would-be Rekha amusingly

repeating the *Umrao Jaan Adaas*, with every little coy flutter and seductive gesture copied to perfection. In between the programmes come the ads promising to teach you *Bharata Natyam*, *Kathak* (a form of north Indian classical dance) and, most importantly, Hindi film dance!

A *Dil Se* or *Raju Chacha* may briefly appear in the top ten films of the week in the US, but it is the ubiquitous Indian store that is the true film lifeline, supplying the latest DVDs and videos along with *samosas* and *mithai*, *masalas* and pickles, *dals* and *pappads*. It doles out food for the body craving spice in the land of the big golden M, and food for the soul yearning for its own brand of cultural sustenance.

A visit to a theatre showing a Hindi film is a planned and eagerly awaited treat. You may have to drive a long way, but the ride transports you back to a remembered – or imagined – homeland. The event is a tribal celebration that transcends political divisions and draws Pakistanis, Bangladeshis, Sri Lankans and others from the Indian subcontinent, almost as much as people of Indian origin.

But it is time to come back home and take stock of what precisely the Hindi film means to

GURU DUTT FILMS (PRIVATE) LTD.
PRESENTS

SAHIB
BIBI
AUR
GHULAM

साहिब बीबी और गुलाम

RK FILMS

SHREE
420

WRITTEN BY
K.A.ABBAS
DIRECTED BY
RAJ KAPOOR
MUSIC
SHANKAR JAIKISHAN

WAHEEDA REHMAN · GURU DUTT · REHMAN AND JOHNNY WALKER

GURU DUTT'S
Chaudhvin
ka
Chand

चौदहवीं का चाँद

DIRECTION M. SADIQ   MUSIC RAVI   LYRICS SHAKEEL

RELEASED BY KAPURCHAND & CO

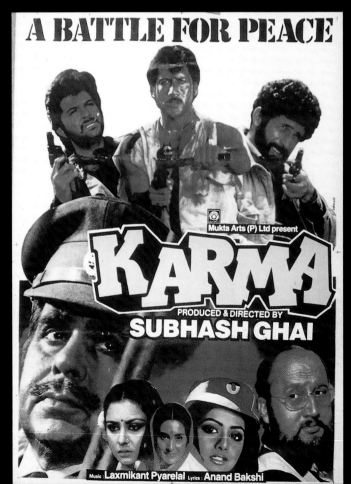

A BATTLE FOR PEACE

Mukta Arts (P) Ltd present

KARMA

PRODUCED & DIRECTED BY
SUBHASH GHAI

Music Laxmikant Pyarelal   Lyrics Anand Bakshi

SHREE 420 and

SAHIB BIBI AUR GHULAM

– all time classics .

CHAUDHVIN KA CHAND

and **KARMA** – blockbusters.

All four movies symbolize the

Hindi film's secular heart.

a nation fragmented by ethnic divisions and regional loyalties. The Hindi film is the all-India film: this is a truism. It is a cementing secular force that heals and binds a contentious, clamorous people. In *Amar, Akbar, Anthony* (1977), the tubes carrying the blood of the three main characters to the blind Nirupa Roy who doesn't know they are her sons – nor do they know they are brothers – are ridiculous by any medical standard. Nevertheless, the heart and guts respond to this symbolic image without asking too many inconvenient questions. Similarly, an earlier age thrilled to Mohammad Rafi singing the plaintive, soul-stirring *bhajan* composed by Naushad Ali: *Man tarpat Hari darshan ko aaj* (My heart yearns for a glimpse of Lord Krishna) and forgot that a devout Muslim was singing a musical composition of another Muslim before a Hindu idol.

There is undeniably a Hindu mainstream consciousness working in Hindi cinema. Some of our greatest directors, poets, actors and technicians have delved into the artistic legacy of a distinct religious identity and enriched cinema with their creativity. What would a Guru Dutt film be without Sahir's poetry? Or a Raj Kapoor film minus its K.A.

Abbas script? One fervently hopes that this life-enhancing trend will continue in our increasingly shrill and divisive times, when 'secularism' has become a shibboleth traduced by the fundamentalists.

Film stars have been the unifying icons in a country starved of role models, particularly in the post-Independence days of cynical disillusionment. Unlike the people of Tamil Nadu, Hindi audiences have not built temples to a star, but this does not mean their fervour

NAYA DAUR

Dilip Kumar – a legendary

icon – and Vyjayanthimala

trying to please Lord Shiva.

Amitabh Bachchan in
his youth.

Posters promoting Madhuri
Dixit, Shah Rukh Khan
and Karisma Kapoor in
DIL TO PAGAL HAI

is any less. I remember how my mother used to speak with awe of Shanta Apte – the domestic guerrilla of *Duniya Na Mane* – and of the way she had inspired a generation of college students to stand up and speak for themselves. The late critic, Iqbal Masud, corroborated this. One of his cherished memories as a student in Madras's Presidency College was receiving, as the honoured guest of their student union, Shanta Apte, dressed in trousers and hat – revolutionary for the 1940s. Dilip Kumar commands a similar respect and the activist Shabana Azmi is heard with attention.

But even more than respect and admiration, there is an element of devotion evident in the frenzy of a crowd to have a *darshan* of its *filmi* deity. It is as if the viewer has transferred to the film star the pious act of feasting his eyes on the image of the chosen god. Even when these tinsel gods have their feet of clay exposed, the abstract idea of viewing them as icons remains undiminished. In a country where the only other icon is the cricketer, the film star fulfils the yearning for a role model – a role model for fashion, if nothing more.

Every decade comes with its own fashion, its own mantra. The 1990s mantra is globalization, invoked with incantatory fervour as if it could magically ease our difficult adjustment to the new millennium. As a nation and a culture, we seem to be experiencing anxiety

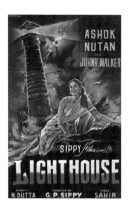

Posters of **LIGHTHOUSE**
and **DO RAASTE**

opposite page
GUIDE
Debonair Dev Anand plays
an amoral guide who is
reluctantly transformed
into a Swami.

GANGA JAMUNA
SARASWATI

Amitabh Bachchan woos
Meenakshi Seshadri.

over the perceived end of our isolation.

The one sure thing in an uncertain world
used to be the ability of the Hindi film to resist
Hollywood's ravaging, global appetite. While
Hollywood carried the American Dream to all
corners of the world, packaging home-grown
genres for both its domestic and international
market, the Hindi film was one of the few lone
rangers holding fast, with unsuspected
strength, to its native territory.

In the 1940s and 1950s our knack for quick
assimilation and creative adaptation made the
western invention a vehicle for forging new
mythologies for a colonized people emerging
into Independence. The Golden Age of Hindi
cinema used the inherited narrative tradition
with imagination, to tell acutely individual
films that could communicate both their
content and form to a wider, appreciative
audience. The young Raj Kapoor Indianized
cinema's most loved universal icon – Chaplin's
tramp – and made Raju the *Awaara* (1951),
the bardic soul of Nehruvian India. Guru Dutt
enhanced the poetry of the *Devdas* myth
with the visual language of an expressionistic
camera and the ecstasy of Christian
martyrdom. Bimal Roy absorbed the lessons
of Italian neo-realism and infused social
awareness into his tender but probing
portraits of Indian life.

Hindi cinema has now lost the moral
edge of its glory days, and this erosion of its
inherent strength has been coupled with a
constant, all-pervasive exposure to western
mass media. It is tempting to see the popular
Indian film as a lethargic *Kumbhakarna* (a
character from the *Ramayana* notorious for his
ability to sleep for long periods) caught

HU TU TU
Tabu (centre) in Gulzar's tale of politics, corruption and betrayal of youth.

MR. INDIA
Sridevi and Anil Kapoor in the biggest commercial success of Shekhar Kapur in the 1980s.

KAHO NA PYAAR HAI
Amisha Patel and Hrithik Roshan made a phenomenal debut in this love story, which was filmed at various locations in New Zealand.

stretching awkwardly in a suddenly constricted space, paralyzed by the spotlight of scrutiny. Has the space for the mainstream Hindi film shrunk just as our collective exposure to the West has expanded beyond the clearly defined limits of the past? The response of the lumbering giant has been fraught with a dual anxiety. First, it has to face the obvious fact that the once faithful audience, even if it has not become really discriminating, has started deserting the formula film all the same. The second factor is more troubling. The purveyor of the popular film seems to have been stricken by self-doubt, by concerns about the validity of the product he has sold for all these years to a largely uncomplaining audience.

However, recent successes such as *Dil Se, Mohabbatein* (2000), *Kaho Na Pyaar Hai* (2000), *Zubeidaa* (2000) and *Lagaan* (2001) offer new promise and excitement. Not with more films shot in ever more exotic foreign locations, but with a return to our roots and our history. Shah Rukh Khan's ambitious epic *Asoka* takes you all the way back to the age of Emperor Asoka, the conquering emperor who embraced pacifism. Aamir Khan's first film as producer, *Lagaan*, returns to the days of the

British Raj and reinvents history with a delightful mix of metaphors. Cricket becomes the means for a subject people to defeat the foreign ruler. As long as the younger breed of stars/producers still dares to back unusual, imaginative subjects, the heart of the movie will beat strongly to a native rhythm. But the Hindi film cannot remain isolationist, marooned in past glories. Too much international water has flown under its picturesque bridges. Native flavours infused with international *élan* seem to be the new *rasa* for a new millennium. Will the *rasikas* respond?

PYAAR ISHQ AUR
MOHABBAT
Romance will always
remain the heart of
Bollywood.

Making Movies in Mumbai

I had just completed a film, *Antarnaad* (1991) that was both produced and distributed by a voluntary organization with individual contributions from its members. This was nine years ago. Soon after, at the suggestion of my long-time collaborator, Shama Zaidi, I was exploring the possibility of making a film based on Dharmvir Bharati's novel, *Suraj Ka Satvan Ghoda* (The Seventh Horse of the Sun's Chariot). Years before, I had given up the idea because the form of the novel had seemed frightfully difficult to bring to the screen. It had ambiguities, simultaneous action on several levels, narrative episodes that telescoped into one another, interiorities that seemed impossible to articulate in the cinema. On the surface, it read very simply: a series of stories narrated by the protagonist to define and illustrate love. But laying it out in a linear fashion would have made it simplistic and banal. Suddenly there seemed a distinct possibility that a television

SURAJ KA SATVAN GHODA, 1992
Amrish Puri and Shashi
Saxena in the film by Shyam
Benegal.

SURAJ KA SATVAN GHODA, 1992

TRIKAL, 1985
With Soni Razdan, Neena Gupta, Magsoom Ali, Sabira Merchant, Anita Kanwar, K.K.Raina and Akash Khorana.

Surekha Sikri in MAMMO, 1995.

producer might actually reduce the novel to a soap opera. I felt that if this happened, the essential worth of the novel, which was largely attributable to its extraordinary form, would be lost. Trying to retrieve the filming rights from the television producer was taking a great deal of time.

It was during this time that I came across a little personal piece in the Sunday edition of the *Times of India*. It was about a woman who had married a man from Lahore and moved there after Partition. On the premature death of her husband, unable to deal with the hostility of her husband's relatives, she decided to return to Bombay to live with her only surviving relative, an older sister. She intended to live the rest of her life in her sister's home. She managed to stay long after her visa expired. When the immigration authorities eventually found out, she was unceremoniously deported back to Lahore, where she had neither a family nor a home. This account was by Khalid Mohamed, the well-known film critic. The woman he had written about was his great aunt. I was deeply moved by this story. It was one of the myriad human tragedies that took place in the aftermath of the Partition of India, tragic stories of families torn apart by man-made borders and barriers. It was an exquisite miniature, and in a microcosm expressed the trauma that had affected the entire subcontinent. I felt that this little piece had the makings of an excellent film. Khalid, of course, had shown no particular fondness for the films I had made. They were often targets of his well-aimed barbs. So I wasn't too sure how he would react to my interest in the subject. My fears, I discovered, were quite unfounded. He even agreed to do the script for the film, which he turned out in record time.

Now came the difficult part. Raising the money to make the film. Until the mid-1980s, raising money for the kind of films I made was easier. We were still in the pre-television era.

Amrish Puri in **SURAJ KA
SATVAN GHODA**

To get screen time in the cinemas was not too
difficult. There was enough of an audience
consisting mainly of the middle classes in
metropolitan cities, whose preference for
cinema entertainment extended beyond the
conventional product turned out by the mainstream industry. There was countrywide television but this consisted of a single channel
owned by the state. With the kind of
programmes it produced, the competition for
cinema was still quite peripheral. Starting in
the early 1970s, some younger filmmakers had
begun to make films that did not necessarily
subscribe to the traditional form of Hindi
cinema in which the use of song and dance
was *de rigueur*. Over time, they had cultivated
a fairly devoted audience that made some of
these films economically viable. Several of
these were funded by the state agency, the
National Film Development Corporation
(NFDC), while individual entrepreneurs
financed others.

For over five years, between 1986 and 1991,
I had been busy doing television and lost
contact with the film business. When I got
back, it was like waking up from Rip Van
Winkle's slumber. Everything had changed.
The non-traditional cinema had lost its entire
audience to television.

When India became independent in 1947,
cinema had already hegemonized the space of
popular entertainment in the country. Two
decades earlier, when movies had become
talkies, Indian cinema had begun to sing. This
had significantly altered its form.

Consequently, it came in for a great deal
of criticism from the art establishment of the
country. No less than Rabindranath Tagore
commented that 'form in art changes
according to the means it uses. I believe that
the new art that could be expected to develop
out of the motion picture has not yet made its
appearance. In politics we are looking for
independence, in art we must do the same.
Every art seeks to find its own independent
manner of expression within the world it
creates; otherwise its self-expression is
undermined for lack of confidence in itself …
no creative genius has yet arrived to deliver
it from its bondage. This act of rescue will
not be easy, because in poetry, painting and
music the means are not expensive, whereas
in the cinema, one needs not only creativity
but financial capital as well.'

Popular cinema was seen as a hybrid,
creatively dependent on the existing urban

preceding page
Nisha Singh, Abha Mishra
in **BHARAT EK KHOJ,**
1988/89.

Harish Patel, Om Puri
and Pankaj Kapoor in
MANDI, 1982.

theatre for its ideas and plots. Although the medium was the cinema, it resembled filmed theatre, complete with frequent interludes of songs and dances. Its success with Indian audiences was undeniable. But this was also its limitation; a kind of procrustean bed that shaped its content to fit its form. On the one hand it had the magpie-like ability to accumulate a great deal of variety to the entertainment it offered, but on the other hand the compulsion to picturize songs and dances in every film tended to circumscribe the subject matter of the films themselves. Often, this form was a hindrance to cinematic self-expression. From time to time, filmmakers would appear on the scene attempting to extend its capacity for self-expression. Among the most notable were V. Shantaram, Fatehlal and Damle, Nitin Bose, Mehboob, Bimal Roy and Guru Dutt. In spite of their exceptional achievements, the form of Indian cinema remained supreme. It was in the decade of the 1950s that Satyajit Ray and, following soon after, Ritwik Ghatak and Mrinal Sen in Bengal, succeeded in giving a new form to Indian cinema. Soon some filmmakers in other regions of India like Kerala and Karnataka made films that created their own kind of

cinema. By the beginning of the 1970s several young filmmakers in Bombay broke out of the mould and made films that were individualistic and attempted to redefine cinema entertainment. I was among those who began making films at this time.

The beginning of the 1990s was a particularly difficult time. Private television channels began to mushroom. By the middle of the decade there were more television channels than you would care to count. The film industry was going into a crisis mode that seemed almost terminal. In order to attract audiences to the cinema, films had to be bigger, brassier, with greater emphasis on size and spectacle, featuring wide-screen formats and digitized surround sound. Raising funds for making non-traditional films, not always easy, now became impossible. It became uneconomical for exhibitors to offer screen time for such films, as they would never be able to fill theatres. The theatres themselves were large, with most of them having eight hundred or more seats. Most non-traditional films were shoestring affairs; small films that did not boast too much by way of production values. Moreover, many of them had little technical polish. The only outlets for such films

Farida Jalal and Sanjay
Batra in **MAMMO**, 1993.

Rajit Kapur in **SURAJ KA
SATVAN GHODA**, 1992.

now were on television channels, but this
did not help to make the films viable since
production costs increased proportionately
after the economy was liberalized. Given
these circumstances, the NFDC had worked
out a strategic collaboration with Doordarshan
(the state television network) to produce films.
Doordarshan retained the television rights
while the NFDC got cinema distribution.

It was this scheme that came to the rescue
of my two film projects, *Suraj Ka Satvan Ghoda*
(1992) and *Mammo* (1995), based on Khalid
Mohamed's script. Both could only be made
on tiny budgets, as the funds available from
the NFDC were quite meagre. All this did not
matter too much to me, as any opportunity to
make these films was better than not making
them at all. But I had a nagging feeling of
unease that the only way these films would
reach audiences was by way of screenings
on television. Prohibitive rentals and large
cinema halls had effectively blocked cinema
release. The lack of audience appreciation
could be very disheartening. This was also the
first time I had made films with funding from
the NFDC. All my previous films had been
made by private producers or through other
ingenious means, with films being financed by

co-operatives that had a stake in ensuring
they reached paying audiences. The greatest
weakness with the NFDC was its inability
to get films into the cinemas. The changed
circumstances due to the television explosion
had made matters worse.

While I pondered over the direction I would
have to take in the future, Khalid came up with
a new script he had written. This was the
story of a *Thumri* singer named Sardari Begum
who had become an unwitting victim of a
Hindu-Muslim riot in the city of old Delhi. It
was a powerful story with the opportunity
to use songs sung in the *Thumri* style.

Films and their songs have always had a
symbiotic relationship. Just as the popularity
of the songs often ensured the box-office
success of a film, equally the success of a film
at the box-office helped to increase the sale of
its music. One of the major developments in
the cinema that accompanied the television
explosion was the growth of the music market.
Earlier, film songs, although very popular,
were not financially very significant for film
producers. By the 1990s this had changed
dramatically. Music rights of films fetched
revenues that could be in some cases almost
thirty to fifty per cent of the cost of making the

A scene from **SUSMAN**, 1986.

film. Predictably, film producers spared no expense in this area. Songs were now picturized in the most exotic locales all over the world. The influence of music videos on song picturization became more pronounced. Often there would be greater stress on picturizing songs than on the rest of the narrative, since the market value of a film depended a great deal on the number of hit songs in a film. It was said that several well-known music composers for films had a repertoire of songs that film producers could buy off the shelf.

I had often used songs in my earlier films. They were there because they were needed as part of the film narrative. I had never thought of them as independent of the film. The exponential growth of the music market had clearly made film songs extremely valuable commodities. Therefore, it was imperative to make the songs of *Sardari Begum* (1996) successful in their own right. The choice of the lyric writer for the songs was relatively easy. I decided on Javed Akhtar who is, arguably, the best Urdu poet among the younger generation of poets today. The music composer was my long-time colleague, Vanraj Bhatia, who had composed the music

for almost all my films over the past thirty-five years. Vanraj is an exceptionally fine composer, well versed in both western and Indian classical forms of music. There is great melodic depth to his songs and his harmonic arrangements are impeccable. However, it could not be said that the film songs he had composed in the past had a mass following. A major reason was that his music had never been promoted with the kind of hype that has accompanied music releases in the last few years.

Liberalization of the economy in the early 1990s brought fresh thinking into the entertainment business. Two corporate entities were floated for the production of entertainment software. One was ABCL, promoted by Amitabh Bachchan, and the other was Plus Channel, who became the producers of *Sardari Begum*. Plus Channel had an ambitious twelve-film project primarily designed for television. As we moved into pre-production, Plus Channel decided to change track. *Sardari Begum* was seen to have market potential even as a cinema feature. This meant a change of scale: wide-screen cinema format, now essential for any film seeking cinema release, camera equipment

Shabana Azmi and Joan
David in **ANTARNAAD**
1991.

with anamorphic lenses, and sets to suit the scale. The cost escalation prevented the use of digital surround sound. So the change did not go far enough. When we finally completed the film, the use of analogous mono sound was seen as an infirmity, particularly in metropolitan cities. Coupled with this was the unaffordable cost of promoting the film. In the event, cinema distribution was dropped and the film was premiered on television. This, it was felt, would help attract audiences to see the film in the cinemas. When the film was eventually released on the cinema circuit, the response was quite feeble. The music of the film, on the other hand, did reasonably well. It was fortuitous that the marketing of its music had been done by the music subsidiary of Plus Channel. The now familiar story was repeating itself. Favourable critical response but no great shaking of the box-office still.

Not until the 1990s was I haunted by the spectre of the marketplace. It had played no part in my consciousness in all the years I had made films. It felt good to banish this ghost when working on three other films during this period: *Making of the Mahatma* (1995), which I had made a little before *Sardari*

Begum, and two others, *Samar* (1998) and *Hari Bhari* (1999), that followed after. The story of young Gandhi covering his South African experience was a co-production between the Government of India and the South African Broadcasting Corporation. I concentrated my attention entirely on the making of the film without concerning myself with its fate at the box-office. The same thing could be said for *Samar* and *Hari Bhari*. The former dealt with a subject that was very much part of my own social concerns. It dealt with the experience of being an outcaste in present-day India, half a century after Independence, which had sought to dismantle the rigidly hierarchical Indian society. The latter dealt with yet another social issue, the rights of women, particularly their reproductive rights. When I decided to cast Shabana Azmi in *Hari Bhari* I remember her mock serious remark: 'When will you stop making these *cause* films and just make a movie?' It is true that cinema is not only a popular art but also a mass art. Making a film to promote any cause is no recipe for box-office success. Yet, somewhere along the way I developed a firm belief that cinema does have a normative role to play in society. It often serves as a platform to initiate,

Rajit Kapur in
**THE MAKING OF THE
MAHATMA** 1995.

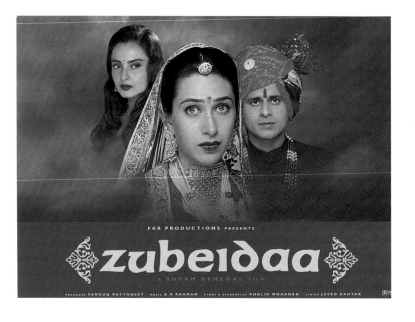

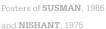

Posters of **SUSMAN**, 1986
and **NISHANT**, 1975

engage and extend public debate beyond its signified role as entertainment. It frequently does more than simply entertain. Films, by their very nature, intended or not, reinforce collective prejudices and have the persuasive power to demonize or ridicule individuals or sections of the community, usually constituting the minorities. A film is largely successful on account of its ability to articulate the wish-fulfilling dreams and the aspirational ideals of significant sections of the population. Because of this power, the normative role cannot be entirely overlooked. This is as good a reason as any I can offer for my choice of film subjects over the years.

In the meantime, with a display of enviable creative energy, Khalid had written two new scripts, one of which, he offered to me. This was a screenplay based on his mother's life. She had passed on when he was still very small. The knowledge he had of his mother was fragmentary. He had lived most of his life with his grandmother who had not been very forthcoming on the subject. His own compelling curiosity had helped him put together the missing links to create the fascinating story of his mother. It had all the ingredients of a grand romance set in princely

India during its terminal decline. To fully realize it as a film, it required a budget much larger than I could usually muster for my films. I offered the first option to Plus Channel. Quite rightly, they felt that the film could only be viable if it had stars, top-ranking actors like Manisha Koirala and Shah Rukh Khan. Manisha, quite predictably, agreed to be in the film. Most female stars would, as the central character of the story was the woman. Shah Rukh did not take long to decline the role. It was the same familiar story with Aamir Khan. It was not difficult to understand why. Both Shah Rukh and Aamir were top stars with a formidable reputation at the box-office. The role offered to them was not the kind that had given them their reputations, male-dominated stories were often written especially for them. After several discussions, Plus Channel pulled out of the project. It went on the back burner and remained there for a couple of years.

At the beginning of 1999, Khalid introduced me to Farokh Rattonsey. Farokh had other business interests, but had made a couple of forays into films in the last twenty years. Disillusioned by the experience, he had sworn never to produce another film. Nothing seemed more unpromising than to meet him.

BLAZE
FILM ENTERPRISES
PVT. LTD. PRESENTS

Ⓐ

Bhumika
EASTMANCOLOR
(THE ROLE)

Produced by : LALIT M. BIJLANI · FRENI M. VARIAVA

Starring :

SMITA PATIL · ANANT NAG
AMRISH PURI · NASEERUDDIN SHAH
SULABHA DESHPANDE
KULBHUSHAN KHARBANDA
BABY RUKHSANA · B.V. KARANTH
and AMOL PALEKAR

Music : VANRAJ BHATIA
Screenplay : GIRISH KARNAD
SATYA DEV DUBEY and SHYAM BENEGAL
Dialogue : PT. SATYA DEV DUBEY
Photography : GOVIND NIHALANI

Direction :
SHYAM BENEGAL

Editing : BHANUDAS
Lyrics : MAJROOH SULTANPURI
VASANTH DEV
Processed at : BOMBAY FILM
LABORATORIES PVT. LTD.

opposite page

Smita Patil in **MANTHAN,** 1976.

Om Puri in **ANTARNAAD,** 1991.

Shyam Benegal on the sets
of **MAMMO,** 1993.

I could discern no evidence of interest even after I told him the story of *Zubeidaa* (2000) which, incidentally, was the name of Khalid's mother. I put it down to the rather lacklustre and desultory effort I had made. If I were in his place, I would probably have reacted in the same fashion. But I was in for a surprise. When it was time to leave, he asked to read the script, which I sent to him the next day. It took another couple of days for him to make up his mind. He decided to produce the film. The question, once again, was how to make the project viable. There would be more money available but not very much more. The script offered an opportunity to use songs and even a dance, since the protagonist in the story participated in a dance number in a film.

A recent phenomenon had been the recognition of major stars as brands. Stars often earned substantial amounts from product endorsements that did not take too much time or effort. They were also frequently offered large sums of money to make appearances or to give short perform-ances, usually song-and-dance routines from one of their films at the numerous film star shows organized by entrepreneurs in India and abroad. These earnings could often rival their earnings from films. One of the reasons for the sudden spurt in star fees could probably be attributed to this development.

I decided to start with a clean slate. In looking for a star who could portray the young, vulnerable yet strong-willed person of our story (the Zubeidaa of our story had died at twenty-two) we zeroed in on Karisma Kapoor. It was ideal casting. What is more, Karisma was also a very accomplished dancer. For the role of the prince, I thought of casting Anil Kapoor. He begged off as he felt he had done several roles of this kind in the past. Khalid came up with the name of Manoj Bajpai. Manoj had recently shot to fame with an exceptional performance as a lumpen underworld character in a film called *Satya* (1999). The role in *Zubeidaa* would be in

Shabana Azmi and
Kulbhushan Kharbanda in
ANTARNAAD, 1991.

preceding pages
Shashi Kapoor and Nafisa Ali
in **JUNOON,** 1978.

Neena Gupta in **TRIKAL,** 1985.

Karisma Kapoor,
ZUBEIDAA 2000.

complete contrast to the abusive, street-smart
gangster he had played in that film. Here, he
was required to play a suave, sophisticated,
polo-playing prince. In real life, Manoj has a
quiet charm and possesses clean-cut looks
and an athletic build. Choosing the star to play
the first wife of the prince was relatively easy.
The perennially beautiful Rekha.

As in *Sardari Begum*, the songs in
Zubeidaa played an integral part. It was
important not only that the music should be
perfect for the film, but also that the songs
should do well on their own. The film was
set around fifty years ago, so it had to have
the flavour of the period without sounding
old-fashioned or anachronistic. The choice fell
on A.R. Rahman, who was not only the most

successful music composer of recent years but
also the most gifted. Recent experience has
shown that the commercial viability of Hindi
films depends on a) the music of the film
attracting a good price, b) reasonable success
in the overseas markets (the growing South
Asian diaspora all over the world shows a
distinct preference for Indian films over all
others) and c) the sale of satellite television
rights. All three of these revenue-bearing
avenues have opened up in the last decade.
The domestic market has shown little growth
since the television boom. Several cinemas
in metropolitan cities have closed down over
the years. Theatre owners and exhibitors,
wherever possible had started to convert the
traditionally large cinema halls into smaller
multiple cinema complexes. For this to happen
in any big way requires not only several
outmoded local laws in each state of the
country to be changed but also a substantial
infusion of capital, which is not forthcoming.
The state governments earn more from the
entertainment taxes they levy on the
exhibition of films than all the sectors of
the film industry put together.

In the present scenario, it was obvious that
one could not rely entirely on the domestic

Nafisa Ali in
JUNOON, 1978.

market to recoup the financial investment involved in the making of the film and its promotion, which was now of fundamental importance. Having factored in all these considerations, we proceeded to make the film. Fortunately, there were no mishaps on the way except when Karisma accidentally sprayed deodorant in her eye! The film was completed on schedule. Rahman wrote an exquisite music score, apart from the hauntingly beautiful songs that he composed to the sheer poetry of Javed Akhtar's lyrics.

Zubeidaa was satisfying in many ways. The film was well promoted. Only two other films of mine had been well marketed in the past and that was over twenty years ago – the films *Junoon* (1978) and *Kalyug* (1981), both produced by Shashi Kapoor. *Zubeidaa* had a worldwide release on the day it was premiered. Its music found its way into the record shops everywhere and the critical response matched that of the audiences.

Almost thirty years after I made my first feature film it has dawned on me that marketing is not just a buzzword. It has now to be seen as a creative extension of film-making. Gone are the days when word-of-mouth could be relied upon to extend the size of audiences for one's films. With mass media growing the way it is, goodness knows how many new information avenues and markets will open up in the present century. In this Tower of Babel, one has to find a way of being seen and heard with the kind of films one makes. A daunting task? Who cares. Onwards now to the next film.

left and above
Scenes from **JUNOON**, 1978
with Pearl Padamsee and
Jennifer Kapoor.

following pages
Jalal Agha, Ismat Chugtai,
Jennifer Kapoor and Nafisa
Ali in **JUNOON**, 1978.

All Time Greats

July 1982. Amitabh Bachchan is grieviously injured while filming a fight sequence for Manmohan Desai's film *Coolie* in Bangalore. India comes to a halt. As soon as it becomes known that he is in Breach Candy Hospital in Bombay, thousands of fans crowd balconies, streets, footpaths, perch precariously on nearby trees, and even clamber up water pipes to get a glimpse of their idol. A collective prayer goes up from every mosque, temple, church, synagogue and gurudwara in India. The Prime Minister, Mrs Indira Gandhi, air-dashes to visit him in hospital. A young girl faints on hearing the false news that her hero has succumbed. The entire country waits with bated breath. And then, finally, their God of the grease-paint world is declared out of danger. India exhales.

Film stars are the hope of India's down-trodden, the very life and breath of a country mired in poverty. They influence the attitudes and the thinking of the masses. The evolution of the very soul of modern India is mirrored in the changing faces of the legends of the silver screen.

Not so long ago, a film career was infra dig for the educated elite. Today, children from educated professional families and scores of Non-Resident Indians (NRIs) throng to Mumbai for a shot at stardom. Newcomer Amisha Patel studied biogenetics at Tufts University in the United States, and then economics, but she returned to India to star in *Kaho Na Pyaar Hai*.

Early Stars – Durga Khote

In the early years few women dared to venture into the world of acting. Those who did tended to be Anglo-Indian, or from families of performers – acting was not considered a 'respectable' career. Durga Khote, who came from an elite Maharashtrian family, was the first to break this taboo. She joined New Theatres to work with legendary filmmaker Debaki Bose and went on to play the lead in early Prabhat films such as *Ayodhya Ka Raja* and *Maya Machinder*.

Durga Khote had an impressive personality and considerable histrionic ability. She played lead roles in many memorable films and then settled down to playing character roles, continuing to work right up to 1980. Many still remember her part as the courageous Rajput Hindu wife of Emperor Akbar in *Mughal-e-Azam* (1960). In addition to being one of the most celebrated actresses of her

PRITHVI VALLABH

Durga Khote played
Mrinalvati, a princess, who
first humiliates the King of
Avantipur, but eventually
falls in love with him.

time, Durga Khote is remembered as the
woman who dared to be an actress and paved
the way for other women of a similar background to do the same.

Prithviraj Kapoor

In the early years, men found it easier than
women to become actors (although it was still
not considered a worthy career for a
gentleman of good repute). One of the earliest
male leads to become a Bollywood legend was
Prithviraj Kapoor.

Prithviraj hailed from Peshawar in the
Punjab (now in Pakistan). His father was a
government officer in the Police Service.
Cutting short his legal studies, Prithviraj
chose to become an actor while still a young
man. He made his debut in a silent film,
Cinema Girl, opposite Ermeline. He also acted
in India's first sound film, *Alam Ara* (1931).
He was strikingly handsome, and fair of
complexion. With these natural attributes, he
seemed tailor-made for the role of the Greek
King Alexander in Sohrab Modi's film *Sikander*
(1941). He starred in numerous other films
including such classics as Debaki Bose's
Vidyapati (1937) and Raj Kapoor's *Awara*
(1951). However, the role that immortalized

him was his portrayal of Akbar in K. Asif's
Mughal-e-Azam (1960). His imperious manner,
extraordinary delivery of dialogue and deep
voice imparted so much grandeur to the character of Akbar, that some critics said the real
Akbar might not have been able to compete.

Prithviraj inspired his sons - Raj Kapoor,
Shammi Kapoor and Shashi Kapoor - to follow
in his footsteps. All of them rose to fame.
Between 1930 and the present, four generations of Kapoors have acted in and directed
films. One of the last films in which Prithviraj
acted was *Kal Aaj Aur Kal* (1971), directed by
his grandson Randhir Kapoor.

KAL AAJ AUR KAL
Randhir Kapoor directed this
unusual saga featuring three
generations of the Kapoor
clan - grandpa Prithviraj
Kapoor, father Raj Kapoor
and Randhir himself.

Shobhana Samarth

An actress who made a breakthrough in the 1930s was Shobhana Samarth. Not unlike Durga Khote, she took up acting as a career when it was still regarded unsuitable for women. Her family's wealth and background might have helped her to break away from convention: her father, Prabhakar Shilotri, was the owner of a bank and her mother, Kantabai Shilotri, had acted in silent films.

Shobhana made her debut opposite Master Vinayak in *Nigah-e-Nafrat* (1935) but won her early popularity playing the female leads in Sagar Film's *Do Diwane* (1936) and *Kokila* (1937). Her roles in mythological films made her a star: as the goddess Sita (wife of Lord Rama) in Vijay Bhatt's *Bharat Milap* (1942) and *Ram Rajya* (1943), a film that related the saga of Lord Rama's ideal kingdom. So powerful was her impact that audiences reportedly showered coins and flowers as soon as she appeared on the screen. A private screening of *Ram Rajya* was even arranged for Mahatma Gandhi, an admirer of Rama's philosophy, though not one of cinema.

Shobhana went on to play the lead role in nearly fifty films. She eventually became a producer, setting up Shobhana Pictures, and directed two films, *Hamari Beti* (1950) and *Chabili* (1960), which launched her talented daughters Nutan and Tanuja (mother of Kajol) as actresses.

K.L. Saigal

The first singing actor of Bollywood who became a legend was Kundan Lal Saigal. He was born in the Punjab and moved from Jammu to Calcutta, where he worked as a typewriter salesman. In Calcutta his singing talent was recognized by B.N. Sircar, who offered him a job at New Theatres. There, he trained under doyens such as R.C. Boral, Timir Baran and Pankaj Mullick. The film that established him as a popular icon was Barua's Hindi *Devdas* (1935). He played the lead role and sang in a voice so soulful and full of pathos, that it had a magical impact on audiences. He also sang and acted in *President*, *Street Singer* and *Tansen*. Saigal's admirers were distraught when he died in 1947, aged just 43, of an illness linked to excessive drinking. Today, he is looked upon as a legendary singer with a distinctive style and voice. No record collection of a true lover of Indian popular music is considered complete without Saigal's geets and ghazals.

STREET SINGER
This was K. L. Saigal's most famous film. It was the debut film of director Phani Majumdar.

Left and below

Devika Rani, a true legend in her lifetime both as an actress and a founder of Bombay Talkies, a studio in the 1930s. After the decline of the studio system in the 1940s she turned her back on Bollywood.

Devika Rani

An actress who won accolades both in India and abroad was Devika Rani. She was born in 1914 to a family of good social standing. Her father was Colonel Chaudhuri, the Surgeon General of Madras, and her great-uncle was the poet Rabindranath Tagore.

Devika Rani's family was progressive enough to arrange for her schooling in England, and she was awarded a scholarship to London's prestigious Royal Academy of Dramatic Art (RADA). It was here that she fell in love with Himansu Rai and married him. Devika first assisted in costume-and-set-design for *A Throw of Dice* (1930). She made her debut as an actress in *Karma* (1933), an Anglo-Indian venture produced by Himansu Rai. The film was made in English and sold as the first Indian talkie with English dialogues. Devika's performance was highly praised by the London press. The Era called her 'a glorious creature, Devika Rani's large velvety eyes can express every emotion'. The News Chronicle and the Star remarked on her perfect English.

The couple returned to India and in 1934 set up Bombay Talkies, which became one of the leaders in the development of a sound film

MEHRBAN, MAHAL,
GUMRAH and PARINEETA.
Ashok Kumar acted in all
four films, which spanned
twenty years of his career.

GUMRAH.

Ashok Kumar with Sunil
Dutt (left), and Mala Sinha
(right). This film was a
story of a woman torn
between two men.

culture. In this Devika Rani played a pivotal
role. She became a film celebrity in Mumbai
with her iconic portrayal of an untouchable
opposite Ashok Kumar in *Achchut Kanya*.

Ashok Kumar

The son of a lawyer and deputy magistrate,
Ashok Kumar Ganguly hails from a Brahmin
family. He started out as a laboratory assistant
at Bombay Talkies and became an actor by
default, yet he remains the longest-reigning
legend of Bollywood. His break came in 1936
when Himanshu Rai cast him as a lead player
in *Jeevan Naiya*, soon followed by *Achchut
Kanya* opposite Devika Rani. The role that
turned him into a star was that of a pickpocket
(Shekhar) in Bollywood's first blockbuster,

Kismet (1943), directed by Gyan Mukherjee.
Ashok Kumar's underplayed performances
created an aura that drew offers from
acclaimed filmmakers such as Kamal Amrohi
(*Mahal*, *Pakeezah*), Bimal Roy (*Parineeta*,
Bandini) and B.R. Chopra (*Kanoon*, *Gumrah*).
His playing of the sophisticated don in Vijay
Anand's *Jewel Thief* and his popular films,
first with Hrishikesh Mukherjee and later with
Basu Chatterji, proved his versatility.

In his biography of the actor the famous
screenplay-writer Nabendu Ghosh writes,
'Ashok Kumar epitomizes the very best in
the craft of acting. He was instrumental
in liberating popular Hindi cinema from
theatricality. He still continues to influence
screen artists.'

ए. वी. एम चित्र

मेहरबान
Mehrban

AVM
PRODUCTIONS

बॉम्बे टॉकीज कृत

महल

अशोक कुमार
मधुबाला

बी. आर. फिल्म्स कृत

गुमराह

GUMRAH

निर्माता वी. आर. चोपड़ा
निर्देशक यश चोपड़ा
संगीत रवि

कलाकार
अशोक कुमार
सुनिल दत्त
शशिकला
माला सिन्हा

अशोक कुमार प्रॉडक्शन्स लि. प्रस्तुत

अशोक कुमार · मीना कुमारी
आशित बरन

शरदचंद्र कृत

परिणीता

PARINEETA

दिग्दर्शक बिमल रॉय संगीत अरुण कुमार

Nurjehan

The Hindustani/Urdu and Punjabi actress and
singer Nurjehan was a pre-Partition legend of
Bollywood. Her rendering of the film song was
so overwhelming that it revolutionized the
genre. The impact of her style in the 1930s
and 1940s was so profound that even the
legendary singer Lata Mangeshkar sang
like her.

Nurjehan started her career as a child
artiste and gained celebrity status with

Dalsukh Pancholi's *Khandaan* (1942). She
learnt music under Ghulam Mohammed
Khan. Her songs in Mehboob's *Anmol Ghadi*
(1946) – '*Aawaz de kahan hai…*' (tell me where
you are…) and '*Jawaan hai mohabbat…*' (my
heart is full of love for you…) – are still popular
with music lovers. Returned to Lahore after
Partition, she remained a leading playback
singer in Pakistan.

Sohrab Modi

Another legend of this period, Sohrab Modi,
specialized in historical period films. The son
of a Parsi civil servant, Modi spent his childhood in North India, where he learnt Hindi
and Urdu. Starting his career in the 1920s as
a theatre actor, he played Jahangir (Hamlet)
opposite Naseem Banu (Ophelia) in *Khoon Ka
Khoon*, a hugely popular Urdu stage play.

Sohrab Modi set up Minerva Movietone in
1936 and went on to produce and direct three
highly ambitious films: *Pukar* (1939), *Sikander*
(1941) and *Prithvi Ballabh* (1943). *Sikander*
was initially banned from being shown in
military areas. Its release came at a time of
heightened political tension – coinciding with
the Second World War and Mahatma Gandhi's
call for civil disobedience– and the censors

AAN

One of Mehboob's first films to achieve widespread distribution in the West, this film was often compared to **QUO VADIS.**

were fearful of the patriotic feelings it aroused.

The Big Three of the Golden Period

The popular cinema in the 1950s and the 1960s came under the spell of three Bollywood stars - Dilip Kumar, Raj Kapoor and Dev Anand. Their films during these decades were entertaining but also socially relevant – the catalysts for social change in post-Independence India.

Dilip Kumar

Dilip Kumar is a legend by virtue of merit. The power of his performance remains unsurpassed. Highly indebted to Bombay Talkies (he was a Devika Rani find), his real name is Yusuf Khan. He made his debut with *Jwar Bhata* (1944) and he made his mark with Mehboob's *Andaz* (1949), as a dashing young man caught up in a love triangle. His restrained performance as a doomed lover in Bimal Roy's *Devdas* confirmed his talent.

Dilip Kumar had the good fortune to work with stalwarts of the 1950s – Zia Sarhadi (*Footpath*), Kidar Sharma (*Jogan*, 1951), Nitin Bose (*Ganga Jamuna*, 1961), Hrishikesh Mukherjee (*Musafir*, 1957) and B.R. Chopra (*Naya Daur*, 1957). Even at the height of his career, he refrained from signing more than

two films at a time, so that he could ensure he did justice to his roles. K. Asif's magnum opus *Mughal-e-Azam* (1960) unfolds the quintessence of his creativity. His performance as an introverted and determined rebel prince puts him quite close to the Emperor Akbar (Prithviraj Kapoor). Perhaps his last defining role was in Ramesh Sippy's *Shakti* (1982), where he played a scrupulous police officer.

Versatility was another of Dilip Kumar's strengths. In addition to serious acting, he excelled in many humorous roles, as in the popular film *Kohinoor*, where he acted opposite an equally hilarious Meena Kumari.

Dev Anand

The matinee idol Dev Anand's popularity remains unrivalled. His contribution to Bollywood as a producer is also immense, through the film company, Navketan, that he set up in the late 1940s. Dev Anand's ambition to join films was inspired by his older brother, Chetan Anand, an innovative Bombay filmmaker whose work included the landmark *Neecha Nagar*.

Dev Anand rose to become the role model for the post-colonial middle class. His 'do-gooder boy-next-door' image, established

A poster of **YAHUDI** Bimal Roy's film starring Meena Kumari and Dilip Kumar.

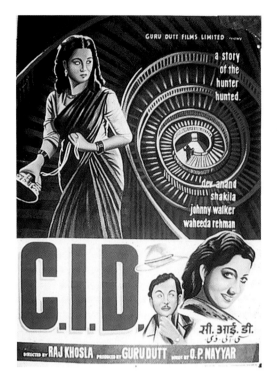

below & opposite
Dev Anand, Bollywood's
matinee idol in different
guises. In **JAAL** *facing
page*, he plays an
unscrupulous gold
smuggler who seduces
the local girl, Geeta Bali.

Posters of **CID**
These hand drawn posters
vividly illustrate how an
artist's perception of a film
can be illustrated so very
differently.

in such films as *CID* (1956), *Nau Do Gyarah* (1957) and *Hum Dono*, made him a hot favourite of the fair sex. Dev Anand was also the first Hindi film actor to add style to stardom. In the 1950s and 1960s he set the trends for the way men dressed. College students had their hair done in imitation of his high puff cut, while his unique way with dialogue – characterized by a rapid delivery of two or three lines in a single breath - was the rage among all age groups. Some critics even drew parallels with Gregory Peck in his performances.

Guide, which he both produced and starred in, remains the highwater-mark of a career spanning more than fifty years. He later took up direction, and in the 1970s made films like *Prem Pujari* (1970), followed by hits such as *Hare Rama Hare Krishna* (1972), *Heera Panna* (1974) and *Des Pardes*. In all these films he played the hero. Dev Anand continues to churn out films with enthusiasm, but none of his recent work has enjoyed box-office success.

Raj Kapoor

The third member of the 1950s trio was Raj Kapoor, who rose to become the biggest showman of Bollywood. Keen that he should

learn the way the film industry worked through direct experience, his father Prithviraj Kapoor motivated him to start off at the lowest rung, as a clapper boy at Bombay Talkies. He then graduated into production work and minor roles. Raj set up his own company, RK Films, with *Aag* (1948). His films possessed an undercurrent of realism, raising issues faced by the marginalized urban poor in post-Independence India. But they also revealed imaginative flair and were highly entertaining.

The film that made him and his female lead Nargis international celebrities was *Awara* (1951). This was followed by *Shree 420* (1955), *Sangam* (1964), *Mera Naam Joker* (1970) and *Bobby* (1973). In his own productions, he reflected an underdog image parallel to

224

Raj Kapoor in **SHREE 420.**
This film is remembered
for its music and lyrics
and was written by the
acclaimed filmmaker
K. A. Abbas.

Posters of **SHREE 420** and **SANGAM.**

JAGTE RAHO

The film focuses on the search for water by a poor peasant who is mistaken for a thief. It won the main prize at the Karlovy Vary Festival in 1957.

Charlie Chaplin, which went down well with the Indian masses.

He also produced the landmark film *Boot Polish* (1954), about the street children of Bombay who are pushed into begging by their circumstances and unscrupulous exploiters.

The success of RK Films often lay in the brilliance of the team members, who included highly creative talents such as the film lyricist Shailendra, the scriptwriter K.A. Abbas and the music director Shankar-Jaikishen.

The mention of Raj Kapoor brings multiple images to the mind's-eye. These include the Chaplinesque underdog of *Awara* and *Shree 420* as well as the urban romantic hero of *Andaz*. But Raj Kapoor gave his best performance of all as the country bumpkin Hiraman in Basu Bhattacharya's *Teesri Kasam*, which was produced by his long-time colleague and friend Shailendra.

Shammi Kapoor

It was not until the swinging 1960s that the dominant trio found itself working alongside certain actors who brought something new into the realm of acting. Ironically, one of the chief harbingers of the change was none other than Raj Kapoor's younger brother, Shammi. Young and handsome, Shammi had started his career in films during the 1950s but each of his films had flopped. Worried that time was running out and eager to get quick results, he is said to have undergone a deliberate change of image and style. Films like *Tumsa Nahin Dekha* and *Dil Deke Dekho* saw the birth of the 'rebel star', an unconventional swashbuckling hero who walked with a swagger, gesticulated wildly as he swung to the tune of catchy upbeat numbers, and acted in a spirit of complete abandon. And the public loved him. By the time Shammi appeared in Subodh

Shammi Kapoor, one of the Kapoor dynasty, with Geeta Bali. He has been a role model for many future generations and is credited for introducing a new style of dance to the Bollywood scene.

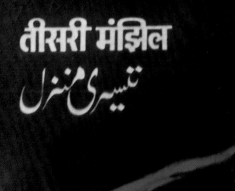

NASIR HUSAIN FILMS PRESENT

SHAMMI KAPOOR
ASHA PAREKH

Teesri Manzil

EASTMANCOLOR

WRITTEN & PRODUCED BY

NASIR HUSAIN

DIRECTED BY

VIJAY ANAND

MUSIC

R.D. BURMAN

LYRICS

MAJROOH

तीसरी मंझिल

تیسری منزل

Posters of **TEESRI MANZIL**, a landmark crime thriller of the mid 1960s.

Posters for **BUD TAMEEZ**, and **KASHMIR KI KALI.** The latter, filmed in Kashmir, featured Sharmila Tagore as a flower girl who captivates Shammi Kapoor.

Mukherjee's *Junglee* (1961), letting out meaningless sounds like 'Yahoo!' and 'Ay yay, ya, Suku Suku', it was clear that the new avatar had received the public's unmistakable seal of approval.

The success of Shammi Kapoor also marked a change of audience mood – an interest in comic relief through leisure activities such as cinema. Later, Manmohan Desai's *Bluff Master* (1963) further strengthened Shammi Kapoor's image. Then came Shakti Samanta's smash hit *Kashmir Ki Kali* (1964), which cashed in on his typical image. Though Shammi Kapoor tends to be viewed as a star to be taken lightly – a player of pranks and monkey tricks - his roles with Asha Parekh in Vijay Anand's superhit *Teesri Manzil* and with Rajshree in *Brahmachari* reveal him as an artiste with consummate skills.

Jeetendra

Another star who soon moulded himself along similar lines was Jeetendra. Introduced by V. Shataram in *Geet Gaya Patharon Ne* (1964) opposite his daughter Rajshree, Jeetendra sprang a surprise in *Farz* where he appeared as a dancing Indian James Bond-type of hero. His famous number '*Mast baharon kaa main*

ashiq' (I'm a fan of intoxicated Springtime) won him the title of 'Jumping Jack'. But he got a chance to present a less frivolous, deeper character in the films he made with Gulzar – *Parichay*, *Khushboo* and *Kinara*.

Fair Ladies of the 1950s

Turning our gaze to female stars, we find that, in the years following Independence, Indian audiences developed a close indentification with Bollywood's leading ladies. They became role models, both as romantic figures and as agents of social change. Nargis of *Awara* and *Andaz* reflected the fire of the modern Indian woman, while Vyjayantimala of *Ganga Jamuna* and Waheeda Rehman of *Pyaasa* and *Kaagaz-ke-Phool* mirrored the pain and aspirations of rural and urban women struggling against the odds. These actresses looked and behaved like ordinary Indian women, but they effectively championed progressive ideas. By appearing conventional rather than militant they enjoyed much greater success.

Nargis

The daughter of actress, singer and filmmaker Jaddan Bai, Nargis was introduced in the film

Jeetendra , called Bollywood's Jumping Jack for his energetic dance steps; here with Babita in a scene from **BANPHOOL.**

AWARA

The intense romantic appeal created by Nargis and Raj Kapoor carried this film's popularity beyond India's shore, making it a huge hit in places like Moscow, Tashkent and Cairo.

Screen Goddess
Vyjayanthimala was a trained classical dancer; her skills were evident in several memorable dance numbers.

Talash-e-Haq (1935). The film that first brought Nargis into the limelight was Mehboob's *Andaz*, where she played a woman torn between tradition and modernity. The film that immortalized her was another of Mehboob's films, *Mother India*, where she played Radha, a woman who fights for the dignity and honour of womanhood, her family and society. After the success of *Barsaat* (1949), Nargis achieved international acclaim alongside Raj Kapoor in the immensely popular *Awara* (1951) and *Shree 420*. In her last film *Raat aur Din* (1967), she played a split personality to perfection.

Nargis was the first actress to seriously take up social activism and was a nominated member of Rajya Sabha, the Upper House of India's Parliament.

Suraiya
Suraiya, who hailed from Lahore (now in Pakistan), was a very different kind of actress. She entered films as a child actress in *Taj Mahal* (1941), and became one of the singing star of the 1950s. This was before playback singing was introduced, and an actress had to sing her own songs. Suraiya had the good fortune to work with famous singing stars and legends such as K.L. Saigal and Nurjehan. She had a beautiful round face, a lovely smile and a voice that combined power with sweetness. Suraiya excelled in historical films depicting the Indo-Persian adab or culture that had developed in northern India during Mughal times. Her singing talent shone forth in the hit film *Mirza Ghalib*, where she acted opposite Bharat Bhushan. She became quite the rage in a different genre of films made with Navketan, playing opposite Dev Anand in *Jeet* (1949) and *Afsar* (1950).

Vyjayanthimala
Another popular actress was Vyjayanthimala, a trained Bharatnatyam dancer from South India. She played significant lead roles with Dilip Kumar in Bimal Roy's *Devdas* and *Madhumati* (1958), B.R. Chopra's *Naya Daur* and Nitin Bose's *Ganga Jamuna* (1961). She was paired with Raj Kapoor in *Sangam* (1965) and with Dev Anand in *Jewel Thief* (1967).

Meena Kumari
The actress who best personified the forbearance of the Indian woman and her upholding of traditional family values was

Meena Kumari. So powerful was this image that she was accorded the title of Tragedy Queen. She had immense dignity and is reputed to have put her very heart and soul into her roles. She had an extraordinary speaking voice, could sing well, and was also an Urdu poetess of some standing.

Her original name was Mahjabeen, which means 'moon face'. Ironically, her impoverished father launched her as a child actress, 'Baby Meena', in a film called *Leather Face*. She caught public attention as Meena Kumari in Vijay Bhatt's musical hit *Baiju Bawra*.

Meena Kumari depicted the role Indian women were expected to play in Indian society. In *Main Chup Rahungi* she chooses to suffer in silence, in *Bhabhi Ki Chudiyan* she is the embodiment of sacrifice and duty, in the classic *Sahib Bibi Aur Ghulam* she is a traditional Bengali woman of a zamindar family who protests against her husband's disregard of her feelings in a way that smacks of feminism without breaking from the traditional mould. Her last film was *Pakeezah*, directed by her husband Kamal Amrohi.

Madhubala

Another star to start off as a child artist was Madhubala. Born in Delhi, she was originally known as 'Baby Mumtaz' in the Bombay Talkies' film *Basant* (1942). She appeared under the name of Madhubala in *Neel Kamal*, directed by Kidar Sharma. Madhubala had a vivacious personality and a sexy look and style.

Her major film of the 1940s was Kamal Amrohi's *Mahal* opposite Ashok Kumar. This was the film that established her, but the film that will go down as her classic is *Mughal-e-Azam*. Here she plays Anarkali, a servant girl in the Mughal court. To give a touch of realism to her performance, and acquire more of the look of a starving, distraught female prisoner, she chose to survive for days on a frugal diet. She was equally adept at portraying light-hearted roles, and is still remembered for her excellent performance alongside her versatile husband Kishore Kumar in Satyen Bose's *Chalti Ka Naam Gadi* (1958).

Waheeda Rehman

Hailing from a traditional Muslim family of Hyderabad (Andhra Pradesh), Waheeda Rehman was a trained Bharatnatyam dancer. She started in regional Telugu cinema but was soon picked up by Guru Dutt for Raj Khosla's

SAHIB BIBI AUR GHULAM
An excellent period film about the decaying feudal system. Meena Kumari plays the traditional house-wife who turns to alcohol in an attempt to re-establish passion in her relationship with her husband.

superhit *CID*. In that film she played a mysterious dancer and an enchanting seductress opposite the debonair Dev Anand. Thereafter, she acted in many Navketan films, which tended to give breaks to fresh talent.

Her best came across in Guru Dutt's *Pyaasa* and *Kaagaz Ke Phool*. In these black-and-white films chiaroscuro is skilfully used to create aesthetic and subtle visual effects, and Waheeda looks absolutely stunning. Her acting had subtlety, naturalness and power. It is sometimes said that the stars of the time were best suited to the medium of black-and-white films. However Waheeda's impact was

not reduced by her appearing in colour. Her performance was particularly outstanding in Vijay Anand's classic *Guide*. Her ability to act as well as her dancing talent found ample scope for expression in this film, where she played against an equally inspired male lead, Dev Anand.

Nutan

One of the most acclaimed actresses of the 1950s and 1960s era was Nutan Samarth. The daughter of actress Shobhana Samarth, Nutan's acting skills were honed by great directors such as Zia Sarhadi, Bimal Roy and

Posters of
SARASWATICHANDRA
and **SUJATA** and a scene
from **ANARI** (below). In all
three films Nutan plays the
traditional Indian woman
whose life revolves around
self-sacrifice and duty.

Hrishikesh Mukherjee in memorable films like *Hum Log*, *Sujata*, *Bandini* and *Anari*.

Nutan had an oval face, and almost perfect features. An extremely expressive actress, she had the ability to convey a great deal through body language and a subdued manner of acting. She personified the grace, beauty and dignity of Indian womanhood as well as her inner strength and power.

She is best remembered for her serious roles. However like her younger sister, Tanuja, Nutan had versatility. She was a good singer, though not in the same league as Suraiya. She also got an opportunity to reveal an endearing and impish side opposite hero Dev Anand and character actor Hirendra Nath Chattopadhyay in the light-hearted film *Tere Ghar ke Samne*.

1960s and the New Stars

In the post-Bimal Roy era, films by Guru Dutt and Mehboob introduced a certain change in the content of films and created new stars. But two actors from earlier decades – Motilal and Balraj Sahni – made a legendary contribution to this change.

Motilal

Motilal Rajvansh, popularly known as Motilal, was perhaps the first star of Indian cinema who developed a natural style of acting. His underplayed dialogue delivery, which looked extremely unrehearsed, was in fact the strength of his performance.

Motilal launched his stamp of acting in S.S. Vasan's *Mr Sampat*, where he played a

CHAUDHVIN KA CHAND
A film that explores the
Islamic practice of purdah;
here in the scene where
Guru Dutt falls in love with
Waheeda Rehman.

gentleman-crook. Later, his role in Bimal Roy's *Devdas* further raised his profile. Motilal's performances in *Jagte Raho* (1956), *Anari* (1959) and *Waqt* (1965) established him as a class apart. The versatile actor Dilip Kumar is said to have acknowledged him as his predecessor.

Balraj Sahni

Balraj Sahni's presence on the screen was absolutely unassuming but very strong. You could never catch him acting. You felt his character. A product of the Government College at Lahore, he initially dabbled in poetry. After teaching Hindi and English at Shantiniketan, he worked for some time for the BBC Hindustani Service.

Sahni's stint with the IPTA (Indian People's Theatre Association) brought him into contact with other creative people, including the Bombay film world. His major break was Zia Sarhadi's *Hum Log* (1951), where he played a frustrated unemployed youth with an emaci-

ated and strained look. Bimal Roy's *Do Bigha Zamin* (1954) was another classic to which he gave his best. Although he was never a star in the traditional sense, his performance in M.S. Sathyu's *Garam Hawa* (1973) was superb.

Sharmila Tagore

A Bengali actress, Sharmila Tagore was introduced to Indian cinema by the internationally acclaimed filmmaker Satyajit Ray. The credit for bringing her to Bollywood goes to Shakti Samanta. Sharmila Tagore shot to fame with *Kashmir Ki Kali*, where she played the lead opposite Shammi Kapoor.

Shakti Samanta's *Aradhana* (1969) reveals her at her best, as a woman who fails to realize her love. She gave restrained but effective performances in Hrishikesh Mukherjee's *Anupama* and *Satyakam*. Her finest work, however, remains Gulzar's *Mausam*, where she played both the lover and the daughter of Sanjeev Kumar.

Rajesh Khanna. During the late 1960s and early 1970s he became one of Bollywood's great movie stars.

ANGOOR

Moushumi Chatterjee and Sanjeev Kumar in a rollicking comedy by Gulzar that illustrated his versatility as a scriptwriter and filmmaker.

Sanjeev Kumar

Originally a Gujarati actor, Sanjeev Kumar soon established himself as a legend of Bollywood. His strength lay in his total commitment to work and the way he internalized his role. H.S. Rawail's *Sanghursh* showed his mettle for the first time when he was pitted against veteran Dilip Kumar.

Sanjeev Kumar could play any role with considerable depth. He remains at the centre of Gulzar's *Aandhi* and *Mausam*. Although Ramesh Sippy's *Sholay* (1975) is a Gabbar film all the way, Sanjeev Kumar is the only other performer who shakes you. In Yash Chopra's *Trishul* he gives an excellent performance as a father encountering his illegitimate son (played by Amitabh Bachchan).

Rajesh Khanna

Rajesh Khanna enjoyed a meteoric rise as a star from the late 1960s up to the mid 1970s. The film that made him a superstar was Shakti Samanta's *Aradhana*, where he played the double role of an Indian Airforce pilot. His

landmark film, the pinnacle of his popularity, was Hrishikesh Mukherjee's *Anand*, where he plays an outwardly bubbly do-gooder who knows that he is slowly dying of cancer.

Despite his status Rajesh Khanna's popularity dipped after the rise of Amitabh Bachchan.

Amitabh Bachchan

Perhaps the biggest life-time legend, Amitabh Bachchan was introduced to films by the leftist filmmaker, Khwaja Ahmed Abbas, in *Saat Hindustani* (1969). He got noticed in Hrishikesh Mukherjee's *Anand*, as a frustrated doctor who wants to serve the people but finds himself helpless.

Initially Bachchan's films after *Anand* did not work till he was cast as a police inspector in Prakash Mehra's *Zanjeer* (1973). Amitabh's angry and sulking persona gelled with the corruption, lawlessness and unemployment prevalent in society at that time.

Talent, hard work and professionalism are said to be at the root of Amitabh's success. The main filmmakers who created his grand image are Manmohan Desai, Prakash Mehra and Yash Chopra.

Jaya Bhaduri

Though her talent had been overshadowed by Amitabh, but when Jaya, with her youthful schoolgirl looks, lovely long hair, innocent face, impishness and infectious laughter, first appeared on the screen in Hrishikesh Mukherjee's *Guddi*, she infused a breath of fresh air into Bollywood. She had an image with which young middle class could easily identify. Her popularity continued for a while and she had a meaty role in *Doosri Sita*, playing a woman so tormented by her husband that she ends up killing him.

Jaya was still a popular actress when she married Amitabh Bachchan. But as Amitabh loomed larger than life on the Bollywood scene, she receded into the background. In recent years she has started re-emerging, following her role as the mother in Govind Nihalani's *Hazar Chaurasi Ki Ma*.

Rekha

An actress for whom pairing up with Amitabh proved propitious, was Rekha. In keeping with typical South Indian actresses of yesteryear, Rekha had a buxom and overfed look when she first arrived in Bollywood. She was also dark-skinned and was regarded more

ZANJEER - The film not only catapulted Amitabh Bachchan to stardom, but also introduced the theme of social protest in a series of films over the next decade.

Rekha recieved the Best
Actress National Award for
her stunning performance
as the courtesan Umrao in
UMRAO JAAN.

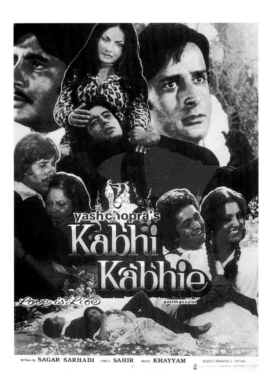

as a sex symbol than a talented actress. However, at some point she decided to refashion herself. By the mid 1970s Rekha had metamorphosed into a slim, extremely attractive and talented actress. Her best performance was in Muzaffar Ali's classic period film *Umrao Jaan*: her stunning looks and effective portrayal of the life and struggles of a courtesan of Nawabi times were acclaimed by the masses and the discerning alike. Rekha and Amitabh became a popular duo with films like *Muqaddar Ka Sikandar* and *Silsila*.

Rekha has matured with immense grace and though now unable to bag the role of heroine, she is still a crowd-puller. She played the queen of an Indian princely state in Shyam Benegal's *Zubeidaa* convincingly and with poise and dignity.

Raakhee

Another actress with immense talent, grace, dignity and soul was Raakhee. Her inward and subdued portrayal of wronged or suppressed women is unmatched. It shines forth in films like Satyen Bose's *Jeevan Mrityu* (1970), Ramesh Talwar's *Doosra Aadmi* (1977) and Yash Chopra's *Trishul* (1978). In *Kabhi Kabhie* Raakhee played first Amitabh

Bachchan's first love. Then she had to submit to an arranged marriage and played the role of a dutiful wife and devoted mother with great poise, realism and sensitivity.

Hema Malini

Projected for the first time on the Bollywood screen as a village belle, in Raj Kapoor's *Sapnon Ka Saudagar*, Hema Malini is an actress of South Indian origin. Her striking good looks and her training as a Bharatnatyam dancer proved great assets. She paired with almost every top actor hero, from Dev Anand, Raaj Kumar, Dharmendra (who she later married), Rajesh Khanna and Jeetendra, to Sanjeev Kumar and Amitabh Bachchan. She

Hema Malini, Raj Kapoor's
dream girl and the suave,
sophisticated Dev Anand,
turned **JOHNY MERA NAAM**
into a blockbuster.

looks gorgeous in *Lal Patthar*, where she is
pitted against Raaj Kumar and a lovely and
gentle Rakhee. She won popularity and had
star value. Epithets commonly used for her
have ranged from the romantic 'Dreamgirl
Hema' to the earthy 'Idli Hema Malini.'
Despite public popularity, she has made a
real impact only in films such as Gulzar's
Khushboo and *Meera*.

Sridevi

Another immensely popular star was Sridevi.
Young, sensuous, energetic and sparkling
with energy, she quickly filled the void left by
the waning of the magic spell cast by Hema
Malini and Rekha. Her first superhit was
Himmatwala, *Tohfa* and *Laadla*. Shekhar
Kapur's *Mr India* was a big success, but it was
films like *Chandni* and *Lamhe* that brought out
the artist in her.

Vinod Khanna

Another star of the 1970s was Vinod Khanna.
He played second lead with Amitabh
Bachchan in *Muqaddar Ka Sikandar*, *Amar
Akbar Anthony*, *Parvarish* and *Hera Pheri*.
Gulzar gave him decent breaks in acclaimed
films like *Mere Apne* and *Achanak*. Another

major hit was Raj Khosla's *Mera Gaon Mera
Desh*. Had he not left the film industry to join
his Guru Rajnish in America, he would have
sustained his rise to stardom.

Smita Patil

A talent of great brilliance whose progress
was cut short by an untimely death was Smita
Patil. A newsreader turned actress, Smita
made a breakthrough with Benegal's
Manthan, where she plays a rural-based
female catalyst for change. Her career's best is
perhaps again a Benegal classic - *Bhumika*
where she plays a role based on the life of the
famous Marathi actress, Hansa Wadekar.

Smita proved to be a far greater success in
mainstream cinema than her closest rival and
friend Shabana Azmi. Her teaming up with
Amitabh Bachchan in *Namak Halal*'s catchy,
earthy and passionate number '*Aaj rapat
jaiye*' (If we slip in the Rain today, let's not
blame each other) became a rage. Smita will
also be remembered for her realistic and
powerful performances in Govind Nihalani's
Ardh Satya, Mahesh Bhatt's *Arth* and Ketan
Mehta's *Mirch Masala*.

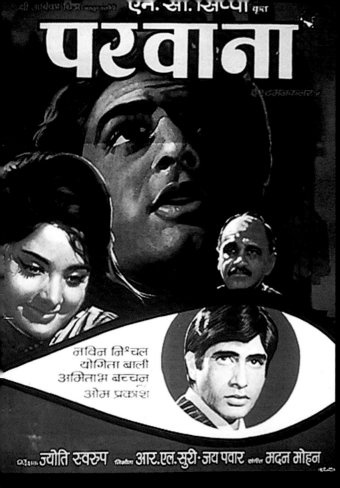

परवाना

नवीन निश्चल
योगीता बाली
अमिताभ बच्चन
ओम प्रकाश

ज्योति स्वरूप · आर. एल. सुरी · जय पवार · मदन मोहन

PRAKASH MEHRA'S

MUQADDAR KA
SIKANDAR

MUSIC KALYANJI ANANDJI

एन. सी. सीप्पी कृत
हृषिकेश मुखर्जी का

चुपके
चुपके

हृषिकेश मुखर्जी · एस. डी. बर्मन
आनन्द बक्षी · गुलज़ार · जयवंत पाठारे

कुली

MANMOHAN DESAI'S
COOLIE

DIRECTED BY
PRAYAG RAJ & MANMOHAN DESAI

MUSIC
LAXMIKANT PYARELAL

Shabana Azmi

A Shyam Benegal find, Shabana Azmi is
one of the most versatile, celebrated and
accomplished actresses of Bollywood.
Heredity has played some hand in her rise,
for her father, Kaifi Azmi, is a legendary lyricist
and her mother, Shaukat Azmi, a well-known
theatre and film actress.

She proved her mettle in Benegal's *Ankur*
and *Nishant*. Opportunities to give expression
to her versatility came pouring in as some
middle-of-the-road directors made films
reflecting the transition that Indian society
was and is still undergoing. Such breaks
include Shekhar Kapur's *Masoom* and Mahesh
Bhatt's *Arth*, where she plays the wronged
wife, and *Ek Pal*, where she is the lonely wife
in a tea estate who succumbs to a past love.
More recently she has acted as a rural
housewife turned unscrupulous politician in
Godmother, and as a married woman who
develops a lesbian relationship in Deepa
Mehta's controversial *Fire*.

Naseeruddin Shah

Two versatile actors of great ability picked by
Benegal to play against actresses like Smita
and Shabana were Naseeruddin Shah and
Om Puri. A product of the National School of
Drama (NSD), Naseer is a polished actor who
masters the minutiae of his roles and delivers
them with great accuracy and naturalness.
His performance in *Manthan* and *Junoon* were
landmarks. His depiction of a Parsi bachelor
in Vijaya Mehta's *Pestonji* is another
masterpiece. An actor who has been
unfortunate not to find enough meaty roles to
work on, he has had to move into commercial
cinema for survival.

Om Puri

Another NSD product, Om Puri's versatility is
remarkable. Be it the role of a man who loses
his power of speech under the shock of the
rape and murder of his wife in *Aakrosh*, an
honest police officer in Nihalani's *Ardh Satya*,
a religious fanatic in Attenborough's *Gandhi*
or a rigid, unbending orthodox Muslim father
in *East is East*, Om Puri could not have done
better. He is one of the rare Indian actors who
has been busy doing roles in international
productions in a big way.

1990s New Generation of Stars

As the last century came to a close, the

LAGAAN

Its Oscar nomination in the Best Foreign film category in 2002 made it the most talked about Bollywood film of the new millenium, transforming Aamir Khan into Bollywood's newest icon.

Shah Rukh Khan and Aishwarya Rai ... contemporary stars who have set trends for the new generation.

Bollywood screen was star-studded - as thick as the Milky Way. We had Salman Khan, Madhuri Dixit, Manisha Koirala, Kajol, Sunny Deol, Aishwarya Rai, Shah Rukh Khan and Hrithik Roshan, to name just the top few. They all seem to have many similarities and little to distinguish one from the other. These are tumultuous times in every sense.

Time creates a gap or a distance and thereby improves our view and vision. It enables us to assess and make well-informed and well-considered pronouncements. At the present moment, we are far too close to the stars of our times to be able to look at the Bollywood players in a balanced way and assess their work.

Of course, if public recognition is taken as a guide, we can hazard some guesses. The star to watch at the moment is Manoj Bajpai. After Ram Gopal Varma's *Satya* and *Shool,* his

frightening presence as a killer in *Aks* speaks of his potential. The same is true of Kareena Kapoor after J.P. Dutta's *Refugee* (2000) and Subhash Ghai's *Yaadein* (2000). Among the female leads, Aishwarya Rai and Preity Zinta have risen in the popularity charts. But to be a star and maintain stardom is like remaining steady in a cyclone. Everything is in flux. Two bad films in succession can easily destroy a career.

While in the new millennium Hrithik Roshan and Shah Rukh Khan bask in stardom, it is Aamir Khan who appears to have had the last laugh with the stunning success of *Lagaan* (2001). It may be premature to predict who among these stars, if any, will eventually rise to the status of legends. If the maxim still holds, of the slow and steady winning the race, it is anybody's guess who's on that track at this point of time.

Villains and Vamps

preceding page
This scene is typical of
a Bollywood film where
tension mounts with
plots and sub-plots.

right
Manoj Bajpai hits stardom
as Bhiku Mhatre in
SATYA.

Premnath: evil incarnate in
NEHLE PE DEHLA

Amrish Puri: always
striking terror.

There is something thrilling about evil. Great men and women who have served humanity arouse our respect, but wicked people do not fail to attract, intrigue and fascinate. When it is a question of seeing evil on celluloid, the impact is even more powerful.

The vamps and villains of Hindi cinema are no exception. Talk to Hindi film-goers, and everyone remembers Gabbar Singh of *Sholay* (1975), Mogambo of *Mr India* and Bhiku Mhatre of *Satya* (1997). Yet the same people might have to scratch their heads to recall the names of the heroes and heroines of these films. Ajit, a top villain of the 1970s, triggered a spate of popular jokes and has several dedicated websites. His fan-following could rival that of many heroic characters of Hindi films.

In the early days of cinema there was a clear demarcation between good and evil. The popular mythologicals, historicals and the costume dramas inspired by folk and Parsi theatres drew much from the ancient Indian epics. The villains were demons, nasty princes, scheming *vazirs* (ministers), arrogant *zamindars* (gentlemen), western-influenced *sahibs* (traitors) – caricatures of evil if judged by modern standards. Ravana was the

AURAT
Kanhaiyalal as the devious
money-lender. This film
was later re-made as
MOTHER INDIA.

Amrish Puri: The face of evil
in **SAUDAGAR.**

epitome of evil, to contrast with Rama's
righteousness. There was no moral ambiguity:
the hero was irrevocably right while the villain
was always wrong, though sometimes he
might be given the opportunity to reform.

Over the years the hero in Hindi films has
not changed much, although the villain has
changed his spots several times over. Good
comes in just one shade of white, while there
is a spectrum of black-to-grey characters who
have been challenging the hero from the dawn
of cinema.

Shah Nawaz, Yakub, Nemo, Jagdish Sethi
and Nayampalli were the popular villains of

the 1930s and 1940s. Yakub was the most
talented and versatile of them all. His most
memorable role was as the outlaw Birju in
Mehboob's *Aurat* (1940) later remade as the
classic *Mother India* (1957).

K.N. Singh can be called the first stylish
villain. He created such an air of menace in
A.R. Kardar's *Baghban* (1931) that he almost
put other villains out of business. So impressed
was Yakub with Singh, that he stopped
playing villains and switched to character
roles. Singh recalled in an interview that in his
heyday villains were always dignified. They
were put in their place by the heroes, but

Kanhaiyalal has always
played a villain that
appeared naive and simple
but the venom was within.
Here in a scene from
HUM PAANCH.

Jayant was one of the most
versatile actors who often
played a villain with style.

below
Yakub : the glib villain.

treated with respect – rarely were there any
terrifying fisticuffs or prolonged rape scenes.
K.N. Singh was usually the classy villain in
suit and hat, blowing smoke rings and
conveying menace with a raised eyebrow
and well-modulated voice. He was a model
for villains to come later – particularly
Shatrughan Sinha.

Villains of the 1950s included Premnath,
who played the cruel prince in *Aan* (1952),
Pran in *Halaku* (1954), *Munimji* (1955) and
Chori Chori (1956), as well as the usual
slimeballs such as Jayant in *Amar* (1954)
and I.S. Johar in *Shart* (1954). These villainous
characters pestered heroines, harassed
heroes, made the lives of good people
miserable and indulged in all kinds of
standard wicked deeds. Yet, easily the most
detestable Hindi cinema villain of the decade
was Sukhilala (played by Kanhaiyalal), the
village money-lender in *Mother India* who
tries to take advantage of the poor and
helpless Nargis. Sukhilala's crude speech,
slimy conduct and clumsy gait became the
trademark of the rustic villain, inspiring
imitators right up to Ashok Saraf's character
of the *munshi* (clerk) in *Karan Arjun* (1995).

The rapacious money-lender, the arrogant

Kanhaiyalal and Pran, it is
difficult to say who is more
wicked. Here in a scene
from **AANBAAN.**

Rahul Dev:
the new face of evil.

landlord and the vindictive dacoit were stock villains in countless rural sagas. Ugranarayan, the wicked *zamindar* played by Pran in *Madhumati* (1958), was the archetype of the haughty, lecherous man who thinks he can get away with anything. Pran also played a fierce dacoit, Raka, in *Jis Desh Mein Ganga Behti Hai* (1960) – a character much copied by later villains.

The very appearance on the screen of these arch villains had a powerful impact on the viewers. Just a sneer or a raised eyebrow from the likes of K.N. Singh or Pran was enough to send a chill down the spines of the audience. K.N. Singh personified the suave gangster such as the sinister hotel-owner in *Baazi* (1951). Recognizing his power, Raj Kapoor gave him another memorable role in *Awaara* (1951). As Jagga, the heartless gangster, he kidnaps a pregnant Leela Chitnis to punish her husband, Judge Raghunath (Prithviraj Kapoor). When her husband becomes suspicious and turns her out of the house, he gives her shelter and brings up her son (Raj Kapoor) to follow him in his life of crime. Jagga was brutal and scary, but still not half as vile as some of the villains who were to come after him.

Kanhaiyalal and Radhakrishna were rustic villains, Jeevan (best known as the trouble-making Narad Muni), Gope and I.S. Johar were comic villains – all of whom fitted quite well into the many social dramas of the 1950s and 1960s, as wicked relatives instigating family feuds.

In the 1950s, film stories left their bucolic settings and moved into the city, which was seen as a corrupting influence on the innocent. In *Pyaasa* (1957), Rehman played the smooth, glib publisher who mercilessly exploited Guru Dutt's idealistic poet. Motilal was the unscrupulous industrialist in *Anari* (1957) who sold spurious drugs and let the honest

Gulshan Grover: playing
the villain in **SAUDAGAR**

Raj Kapoor take the rap. The protagonist of *Taxi Driver* (1954, Dev Anand) was exposed to the ugly underbelly of the city, while the pure-hearted hero (Raj Kapoor) of *Shree 420* (1955) was drawn into a scam to cheat poor slum-dwellers.

In the 1950s, when Hollywood gangster movies and *noir* thrillers influenced film-makers like Chetan Anand, Guru Dutt, Raj Khosla and Shakti Samanta, the villains in the films were gangsters, dishonest businessmen, night-club owners or smugglers. They wore shiny suits and western-style hats, smoked and drank excessively and had molls on their arms. The notorious villain's den, with revolving doors and garish décor, was also a familiar feature in many films, as were fight scenes set in godowns and strange-looking warehouses. When K.N. Singh, Bir Sakhuja, Madan Puri, Pran, Sapru, Jeevan or Tiwari came on screen, audiences knew they were villains, and they were also sure that these scoundrels would come to no good in the end.

Pran's image as a baddie was so entrenched in the popular psyche that people stopped naming their sons Pran. Most actors who played villains did so when their careers as heroes did not take off. Since they played

strictly bad characters, they were straitjack-eted in their roles to the point of being reviled by people offscreen. Prem Chopra, who has had a very long career as a baddie, recalled how he accepted his first role as villain with great reluctance. For many years, he did not allow his daughters to watch his films because he was afraid of what they would think of him! His social life was in tatters because people would shy away from being seen with a man who did such awful things on screen. The screen villains – Kanhaiyalal, Madan Puri, Sajjan, Rehman, Jeevan and others – found that incensed audiences would confuse reel life with real life, believing that if a man was bad on screen, he must be bad in everyday life too.

Gulshan Grover was another actor who forbade his son from seeing his films, lest he be upset by the sight of him getting a bashing from the hero. His mother was so distressed by his vile antics on screen that she was afraid of facing her acquaintances when she went to the temple, and begged him to give up acting and return home! Grover related how he once provoked an interminable delay on a flight when he was allocated the last available seat, usually reserved for the crew. A tearful

Gulshan Grover has been one of the most popular villains of the 1980s and 1990s.

Prem Chopra. He achieved stardom by playing a lecherous and creepy villain.

airhostess refused to sit next to him – she would quit, she said, rather than share a seat with a villain.

Villains sometimes played special roles. Rehman, in particular, acted in some really complex parts. In *Sahib Bibi Aur Ghulam* (1962), directed by Abrar Alvi, he is a *zamindar* whose neglect drives his wife to drink. He and his brother, another famous villain Sapru, are however portrayed as products of a decadent feudal system, incapable of breaking away from inherited patterns of behaviour. In *Yeh Raaste Hain Pyar Ke* (1963) Rehman played a 'charmer' who rapes his best friend's wife (Leela Naidu).

Prem Chopra, a most reluctant villain, found his career taking off in a big way with *Do Raaste* (1969), where he played the selfish brother who is led astray by his wife, Bindu. He abandons his family to chase material wealth, ambition and individualism (all considered undesirable traits in those days). In Manoj Kumar's *Upkaar* (1967) he played the bad city-educated son who is nasty to his mother and his farmer brother. In a family-centric culture, a son or brother who wants a *batwara* (division/separation) is allotted first place in the most-hated list even to this day.

In the recent *Ek Rishta* (2001), the villain was the wicked son-in-law (Mohnish Behl) who cheats his wife's (Juhi Chawla) parents and breaks up the family.

Upkaar is also notable because it marks an about-turn in the career of Pran, the dominant villain of the 1950s and 1960s. One minute he was whipping a cowering Dilip Kumar in *Dil Diya Dard Liya* (1966) and *Ram Aur Shyam* (1967), the next he was playing a good character, Malang Chacha. Audiences found the transformation hard to believe and cringed every time he came on the screen. Pran was, however, lucky to be given opportunities for shedding his negative image. He played a truly funny role with Ashok Kumar and Om Prakash in the hugely comic *Victoria No 203* (1972). Again, in *Zanjeer* (1973) Salim-Javed created for Pran the role of a Pathan who gives up his criminal ways to stand by the hero, Amitabh Bachchan. The number that he sang, *Yaari Hai Imaan Mera* (Friendship is my religion), became a hit. Generally, other villains did not have the good fortune to manage mid-career switches. Pran's seniors and contemporaries – K.N. Singh, Madan Puri, Jeevan, and Kanhaiyalal – worked in films for years but could not shake off their 'villain' tag.

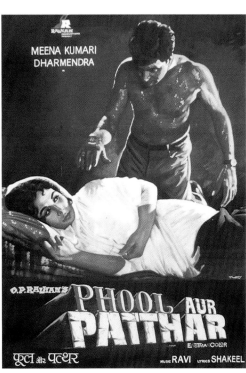

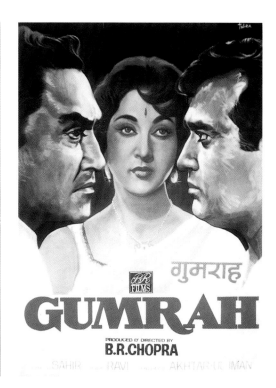

The anti-hero had made a tentative entry into Hindi films with the 1943 superhit *Kismet*, in which Ashok Kumar plays a character who turns out all right in the end. Years later, he also played a surprisingly devious rogue in *Jewel Thief* (1967). Dev Anand played another attractive blackguard in Guru Dutt's *Jaal* (1952). If the villains reformed in the end, and the heroines forgave them, they were pardoned by the audiences too. Sunil Dutt played the rebellious Birju who is shot down by his mother in *Mother India*; he then went on to play the negative character of a dacoit in *Mujhe Jeene Do* (1963) – a criminal without a cause who the director, Moni Bhattacharya,

nonetheless treats with sympathy. Dilip Kumar played an outlaw in the Nitin Bose classic *Ganga Jamuna* (1961); we see him suffering at the hands of a predatory *zamindar (*Anwar Hussain) and feel pity for him when he is shot dead by his brother, an honest cop (Nasir Khan).

Somewhere down the line, evil in society overtook evil in films. By the 1970s neither Birju of *Mother India* nor Ganga of *Ganga Jamuna* would be considered bad. Today's audiences, accustomed to their heroes being murderers, gangsters and psychopaths, would consider such outlaws to be quite tame in comparison. Javed Akhtar of the Salim-Javed

Posters of **KANOON**, **PHOOL AUR PATTHAR** and **GUMRAH**, hand-painted by talented painters in Mumbai.

Om Puri: internalized
violence.

Om Puri: internalized violence.

team, who with *Zanjeer* created the angry
young man persona for Amitabh Bachchan,
has remarked that there was a spurt in crime
and lawlessness during and after the
Emergency rule in India (1975). The petty
crooks and the small-time gold-smuggling
gangs were replaced by a large, well-organ-
ized underworld with its own codes and rules.
There was a collective loss of innocence.

The subject of rural exploitation was
treated with terrifying realism in Shyam
Benegal's *Nishant* (1975) and in Govind
Nihalani's *Aakrosh* (1980). In the latter the
tribal male, played by Om Puri, learns that
he can never get justice while his opponents
are powerful people, and he internalizes his
violence by turning it on himself.

At the same time, the urban scenario was
changing rapidly. The urban 'hero' would not
make a virtue of suffering, poverty or truth.
He began to fight back, taking the law into his
own hands if he had to, and killing without
qualms. In Yash Chopra's *Deewaar* (1975),
Vijay (Amitabh Bachchan) is traumatized as a
child when his innocent father is framed and
he has *mera baap chor hai* (my father is a thief)
tattooed on his arm. But unlike his mother
(Nirupa Roy) or brother Ravi (Shashi Kapoor),
he refuses to accept injustice. To avenge
his family's suffering and to amass wealth,
he takes to crime. Vijay's loss of principles
clashes with Ravi's duty as a policeman. He
is shot dead by his brother and dies in his
mother's lap. At the time the film was made,
it was inevitable that a man who went astray
would be punished. A few years later, even
this certainty was dropped.

The 1970s saw the emergence of some
quite unusual and extremely vicious villains.
Perhaps for the first time, a villain became
more popular than the hero of a film. Gabbar
Singh of *Sholay* – played by Amjad Khan, the
son of actor Jayant, a well-known villain and
character actor – is a movie legend.

Gabbar Singh was pure evil simply for the

sake of it, and not because he had a grievance against the 'system', or a reason to become a bandit. His brand of sadism – cutting off the arms of the Thakur (Sanjeev Kumar), shooting three of his men after making them believe they had survived his version of Russian roulette, or making Basanti (Hema Malini) dance on broken glass – was entirely new. Villains had killed, raped and maimed in the past, but never with such undisguised glee. Even his dress was different. Whereas earlier dacoits had worn *dhotis*, he had a novel get-up of army fatigues, military boots, bandolier, rough stubble and tobacco-stained teeth. Amjad Khan went on to play other villainous, comic and character roles, but nothing he did

ever matched the magic of *Sholay*.

Another sophisticated villain entered the scene. Ajit had had his run as leading man and played an ambiguous character in B.R. Chopra's *Naya Daur* (1957) – that of a man who goes against his friend (Dilip Kumar) in the mistaken belief that he has been betrayed – but he got his second wind with *Yaadon Ki Baraat* (1973) and Prakash Mehra's *Zanjeer,* in which he played a strong foil to Amitabh's brooding inspector, as a man seeking revenge for the murder of his parents. In Subhash Ghai's *Kalicharan (*1976), when he drawled '*Saara shaher hamen lion ke naam se jaanta hai*' (the entire city knows me by the name of Lion), he could not have imagined he was

Gabbar Singh became the iconoclastic villain of the century for his performance in **SHOLAY**.

Danny Denzongpa torturing

Zeenat Aman in

B.R. Chopra's **DHUND**

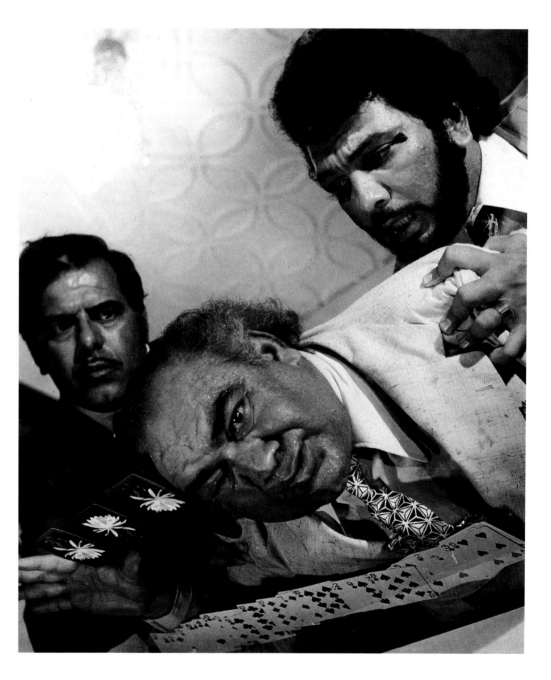

ensuring his own immortality. So popular did the trio of the boss Lion and his accomplices Raabert and Mona become, that they featured in endless jokes. Interestingly, Ajit's character in *Naya Daur* was the model in the recent hit *Lagaan* (2001) for the villain Lakha (Yashpal Sharma), whose jealousy leads him to betray his side.

Premnath, another leading man of his time who had switched to villainy, got to play a perverted criminal in Vijay Anand's *Johny Mera Naam* (1970). In the most shocking scene, he makes Padma Khanna do a striptease while he orders the killing of her boyfriend.

By contrast, Shatrughan Sinha, blowing smoke rings and talking in a cheerfully bombastic style, played a rather likeable villain in *Rampur Ka Laxman* (1972). Along with Vinod Khanna, the horse-riding dacoit of *Mera Gaon Mera Desh* (1971), he was one of the very rare actors popular enough to make a successful changeover from villain to hero.

Yet another great villain made his appearance in the early 1970s – Danny Denzongpa in B.R. Chopra's *Dhund* (1973). It was his first major role and marked the success of his struggle to get film producers to accept

his Sikkimese looks. Relishing the break, he very convincingly played the memorable part of a savage and disabled husband who, though constantly in a wheelchair, tortures his wife (Zeenat Aman).

The release of *The Godfather* (1972) changed the image of the criminal. The Mafia Don was no longer a figure to be condemned, but was to be feared and respected. His

Premnath as the Indian
Godfather in **DHARMATMA.**

Ranjeet plays the bad guy
in **SHARARAT.**

Raj Babbar attacks Zeenat
Aman in **INSAF KA TARAZU**.
Raj Babbar plays a
sophisticated but
dangerous rapist.

power was immense, spreading through and corrupting the police force, the film industry and the government. Inevitably, echoes of *The Godfather* were heard in Hindi cinema. Feroz Khan's *Dharmatma* (1975), was a direct lift, while his *Dayavan* (1988), a remake of Mani Ratnam's powerful Tamil film *Nayakan* (1997) starring Kamal Haasan, was an obvious tribute.

By the 1980s, films could not keep pace with the violence of everyday society – with the corruption, political skulduggery and the seeds of terrorism. No scriptwriter, however doped out, could have cooked up a fiction as horrific as the Bhagalpur blindings, in which the police poured acid into the eyes of so-called criminals in a travesty of speedy justice. People had lost faith in law-enforcers and politicians. There did not seem to be any positive role models. TV, followed by video, brought about a crisis for the industry. A large chunk of the middle-class audience was lost. Films increased their quotient of violence, sex and sensationalism in an attempt to lure a predominantly male audience into the cinema halls.

In *Insaaf Ka Tarazu* (1980), the rape scenes of Zeenat Aman and an underage Padmini

Kader Khan: comic villain in
David Dhawan's **HASINA
MAAN JAYEGI.**

above right
Sadashiv Amrapurkar: the
menacing villain.

opposite
Naseeruddin Shah as the
villainous Wazir in
RAAJKUMAR.

opposite below
In **TEHELKA**....Amrish Puri
plays Dong

Kolhapure were picturized in sickening detail, but the audiences enjoyed them. Raj Babbar, who played a depraved rapist, was quite amazed to receive tons of fan mail. Rape became a regular ingredient in the commercial *masala* film. Far from being frightened of the villains, the audience was dazzled by their aura of strength and power. When Rama Shetty (Sadashiv Amrapurkar) made his appearance in Govind Nihalani's *Ardh Satya* (1983), audiences were almost rooting for him over the upright self-doubting hero (Om Puri). A jovial, pragmatic and powerful don, operating out of a seedy gambling den and pulling strings in the corridors of power, he was a man who commanded fear and admiration in equal measure.

In this decade of mayhem, Gulshan Grover made an impact as the molester of the retarded Sridevi in *Sadma* (1983). Nana Patekar, who made a career out of playing dysfunctional characters, made his debut in *Aaj Ki Awaz* (1984), in which Raj Babbar turns vigilante after his sister is subjected to a brutal rape.

In films coming out of the growing studios of Hyderabad, the comic villain made a reappearance in an attempt to leaven the overt crudity. Kader Khan and Shakti Kapoor formed a team that lasted the decade – in *Himmatwala* (1983), *Mawaali* (1983), *Tohfa* (1984) and other films.

Films began to be made on the theme of urban youth disillusioned by the system and resorting to violence. In *Arjun* (1985) Sunny Deol played a *chawl* (tenement) boy conned into wrongdoing by a smooth-talking politician (Anupam Kher). N. Chandra examined unemployment and crime in an offbeat setting in *Ankush* (1986) and *Tezaab* (1987) – precursors of films like *Satya*.

The outbreak of terrorism prompted the creation of the villainous Dr Dang (Anupam Kher) – in *Karma* (1986) – who wants to destabilize the country. The comic counterpart to Dr Dang was Mogambo in *Mr India* – the garishly dressed, clownish megalomaniac with a ridiculous catchphrase, '*Mogambo Khush Hua'* (Mogambo is happy). Mogambo, played with over-the-top funkiness by Amrish Puri, became very popular with children and is presently the villain most instantly recalled after Gabbar Singh of *Sholay* fame. Both have been used to sell products as varied as biscuits and mosquito repellent mats.

Naseeruddin Shah also played a cartoon

Amrish Puri in **DIVYA
SHAKTI.**

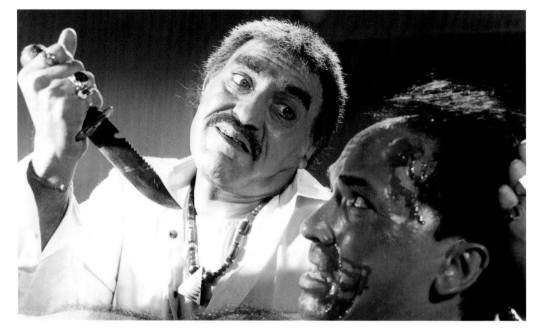

Naseeruddin Shah and
Mukesh Tiwari on the sets
of a Rajkumar Santoshi film
CHINA GATE.

villain in Ketan Mehta's colourful *Mirch Masala*
(1987), chasing Smita Patil all over the village.
But evil could no longer be taken lightly. The
villain of *Parinda* (1989) was a taster of the
way villainous fare would be doled out in
the future. Up to then there had been little
ambiguity about right and wrong. If Sunny
Deol took to the gun in *Arjun*, *Dacait* (1987)
or *Yateem* (1989), he had good reason to do so.
But in *Parinda* the 'heroes' (Jackie Shroff
and Anil Kapoor) are both gangsters and
killers. The villain is Anna (Nana Patekar),
a psychopath who kills his own wife and
child and has not a streak of humanity in him.
Everyone is bad.

    Dayavan (1988) told the story of a boy
who kills a corrupt policeman (Amrish Puri)
who had made life miserable for poor
slum-dwellers. Escaping to Mumbai and the
labyrinthine slums of Dharavi, he finds shelter
with a man who is a crook but a good,
god-fearing man. He becomes the protector
of the area - in Mumbai lingo he is a Dada, the
Indian equivalent of Godfather. He is a criminal and a killer, but he also helps the
poor, rescues a prostitute and provides for
the family of the cop he killed. Is he a villain?
Is he a hero?

This was the grey world that films would
increasingly portray in the 1990s. Amitabh
Bachchan had steadfastly stood for what was
right and just, even when he killed evil-doers
in films such as *Andha Kanoon* (1983) and
Inquilab (1984). But then he played a Mafia
Don in *Agneepath* (1990), leaving no one who
could reassure confused audiences about
Good and Evil.

    Corrupt politicians, sadistic cops, remorse-
less rapists, gangsters, hitmen, extortionists,
terrorists and mass murderers – these villains
proliferated in the 1990s, both in real life and
in films. Some villains took the menace out of
the characters they played by adopting comic
get-ups, quirks or catchphrases. They seemed
to say: Don't take us too seriously, people;
there are plenty of others in the real world who
are far worse than us – watch out for them!

    In *Sadak (*1991) Sadashiv Amrapurkar
played Maharani, a fierce brothel-running
eunuch, with a mixture of humour and
menace, that audiences seemed to appreciate.
In *Tehelka* (1992) Amrish Puri played another
cartoon-villain, Dong, with the silly catchphrase '*Dong Kabhi Wrong Nahin Hota*' (Dong
is never wrong). Om Puri played a manic don
in *Narasimha* (1991) and a crude politician and

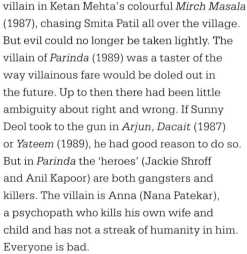

rapist in *Purush* (1993). Anupam Kher was an effeminate villain *in Mast Kalandar* (1992), Aditya Panscholi a cocaine-snorting gay mobster in *Saathi* (1991), Danny Denzongpa a devoted family man and gangster in *Hum* (1992). In *Sir* (1993) Gulshan Grover played Chappan Tikli, a gangster with a loony family and Paresh Rawal was the kind mafia don in the same film.

As a wider audience returned to the cinema, a great deal of imagination went into creating a variety of credible bad men. Milind Gunaji was a frustrated *zaminda*r in *Virasat* (1997), Mohan Joshi was a realistic small-town fixer in *Mrityudand* (1997), Nana Patekar was a Bangladeshi war veteran who tortures his wife in *Agnisakshi* (1996), Ashutosh Rana played serial killers in *Dushman* (1998) and *Sanghursh* (1999), and Akshay Kumar played a killer reformed by a child in *Jaanwar* (1999).

The villain of the decade, however, was Shah Rukh Khan who played a crazed killer in *Baazigar* (1993), a stalker in *Darr* (1993) and a spoilt, rich, demented playboy in *Anjaam* (1994). He played these characters so unapologetically, with no hesitation and with such an air of injured innocence, that audiences actually applauded when he threw

Shilpa Shetty to her death in *Baazigar*, or terrified Juhi Chawla out of her mind in *Darr*. They didn't hate this guy, they weren't afraid of him – rather, they turned him into the biggest star of his generation. Shah Rukh, playing characters that were almost proud of being evil, set a trend for heroes to play a negative role at least once in their careers.

Sunny Deol, the convincing underdog of *Ghayal* (1990), *Damini* (1993) and *Ghatak* (1996), played a criminal in *Jeet* (1996) and *Arjun Pandit* (1999). Similar role reversals were made by his brother Bobby Deol in *Bichhoo* (2000) and *Badal* (2000), by Sunil Shetty in *Hu Tu Tu* (2000) and *Dhadkan* (2000), Govinda in *Shikari* (2000) and Saif Ali Khan in *Kya Kehna* (2000). Jackie Shroff played completely black characters in *Mission Kashmir* (2000) and *Farz* (2001), almost resurrecting his flagging career in the process. Sanjay Dutt played a series of criminals and sociopaths – *Khalnayak* (1993), *Kartoos* (1999), *Jung (*2000*)*, *Khauff* (2000)*, Baaghi* (2000) and *Vaastav* (1999) – for which he won best actor awards. Despite this long record of villainous roles, he is still considered a 'hero'. Similarly, Nana Patekar played characters with a maniacal edge in *Parinda, Agnisakshi, Krantiveer* (1994),

Ghulam-e-Mustafa (1997) and *Wajood* (1998) with no appreciable decline in his popularity.

One notices a shift in the way normally negative roles were conceived in typical Bollywood films. It was Mani Ratnam's *Roja* (1992) that looked the problem of terrorism right in the eye, and wove it into an engrossing story – with songs and all – about the travails of a simple village girl whose husband is kidnapped by militants in Kashmir. The leader of the gang, played with intelligence and humour by Pankaj Kapoor, is an educated man with a mission, who argues rationally with his hostage. If this was the face of evil, as opposed to a singing-dancing muscular hunk, then it was a frightening one. Strangely, the off-mainstream *Drohkaal* (1994) by Govind Nihalani also had a bespectacled, intellectual terrorist who manipulates the lives of top cops from his prison cell, played with chilling intensity by Ashish Vidyarthi, and in *Thakshak* (1999) there was the deranged gangster Sunny (Rahul Bose), who is educated enough to recite Nehru's Tryst with Destiny speech and subvert it.

Where parallel cinema leads, commercial cinema is quick to follow. Sanjay Dutt played a militant in *Khalnayak* (1993) – he did not need to have a cause or an ideology, but had only to look mean and menacing and to shoot straight. In *Diljale* (1996) Ajay Devgan plays a terrorist who has been victimized by the system, but his fight is conducted from a lavish set, complete with a female terrorist doing seductive song-and-dance numbers. The hero (Bobby Deol) of *Badal (*2000) is really a character out of Gulzar's *Maachis* (1996), placed in a mainstream set-up where, along with the usual *naach-gaana* (song-and-dance*)* he pursues a personal vendetta – to kill the cop responsible for slaughtering his family. The portrayal of the cop (Ashutosh Rana) as a caricature monster increases our sympathy for Badal's militant activities.

Interestingly, the chief of the gun-running operations in *Sarfarosh* (1999) is a Pakistani *ghazal* singer (Naseeruddin Shah) loved and respected in both countries. *Pukar* (2000) with a dedicated armyman as hero (Anil Kapoor), also played the patriotism card but turned the villain Abroosh (Danny Denzongpa) into a growling and grimacing, totally outlandish creature.

In *Farz* Jackie Shroff (who started his career as a villain's sidekick in *Swami Dada* (1982), plays a character called Gawa Firozi.

Posters of **BAAZIGAR** and
PARINDA.

Hrithik Roshan in **MISSION
KASHMIR**. He plays the
role of a terrorist in this film
which focuses on the
hostility between India and
Pakistan over Kashmir.

He is a terrorist, drugs and arms dealer and explosives expert who looks like an absent-minded professor but has an evil brain behind the mild bespectacled look.

In *Mission Kashmir* (2000) Jackie played an Afghan terrorist Hilal Kohistani, wild eyes rimmed with kohl and a maniacal look that could send a chill up the spine of a faint-hearted viewer. Current superstar Hrithik Roshan, just three films old, has already portrayed a terrorist in two of them, *Fiza* (2000) and *Mission Kashmir* – a very attractive one at that.

The gangster has followed the same trajectory to cinema respectability. In *Satya* Bhiku Mhatre (Manoj Bajpai) laughs non-stop and shoots people at point-blank range. He enjoys his power and inducts the protagonist Satya into his world – no justification is offered for these choices, no explanation, no remorse. Manoj Bajpai in the recent *Aks* (2001) gets to play the ultimate villain – a dark indestructible representative of evil whose soul lives on in the bodies of others when he is killed, implying that evil can never be completely destroyed, no matter how strong the forces of good (Amitabh Bachchan) may be.

Vaastav (1999) has a *chawl* boy turned

gangster (Sanjay Dutt) cheerfully showing his gun and his gold to his stunned parents. *Bombay Boys* (1999) has a gangster (Naseeruddin Shah) who is clearly demented and enjoys spearing lizards on the wall. Twenty years ago these characters would have been villains, now they are there for the viewers' amusement.

Villains have been becoming more realistic and frightening over the last few years, and films were talking of the underworld-police-terrorism nexus before it was taken up by the newspapers and TV. What was once dismissed as *filmi* (unrealistic) exaggeration, now seems horrifyingly true. Between terrorism, politics and the underworld, the villain, the anti-hero and other negative characters have their work cut out for them. The fun of chasing them pales when there are guns, bombs, gizmos and governments to play around with.

If the rogues' gallery of villains is rich and full to overflowing, the vamp has been given short shrift in Hindi films. Just as the leading lady in post-1960s cinema was relegated to decorative purposes, the vamp is not accorded half as much importance as the villain.

A REASON TO LIVE
TAX FREE

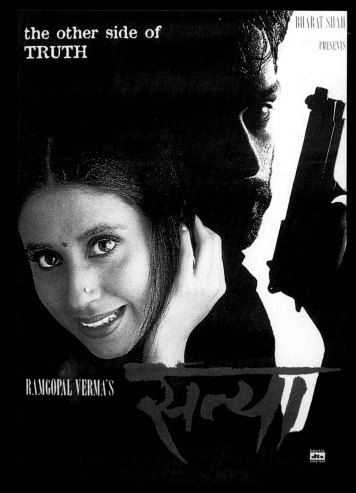

the other side of
TRUTH

BHARAT SHAH
PRESENTS

RAMGOPAL VERMA'S

Shabana Azmi in **GODMOTHER**. Shabana plays a rural housewife whose husband is murdered. Initially manipulated by powerful politicians, she later turns the tables on them.

Vamps

In terms of characterization, the vamp in Hindi films has always been someone who does not abide by tradition. She is either the head-strong woman who does not fit into the joint family, does not obey her husband, does not serve her in-laws, the woman who is not an ideal wife and mother. Or she is the cour-tesan/prostitute who leads fine men astray. Or the other woman who breaks up a family. In nearly all films and stories rooted in Indian reality, women have to be antagonistic towards each other in the joint family set-up. The *saas-bahu (*mother-in-law/daughter-in-law)*, jethani-devrani* and *nanad-bhabhi* (other female relatives in a joint family*)* are traditional enemies. If they get on well, there is nothing exciting or dramatic. And then there is the classic *patni-sauten* (wife-other woman) relationship, which can hardly be anything but acrimonious.

A typical vamp in Indian films is the wicked mother-in-law, played in countless films by Lalita Pawar, whose career as a leading lady was ruined when a slap during the shooting of a film left her face slightly disfigured. In V. Shantaram's *Dahej* (1950) she was the mother-in-law from hell who put her hapless daughter-in-law through all kinds of torture for the crime of not bringing enough dowry. Lalita Pawar played the entire repertoire of wicked women. In *Mr and Mrs. 55* (1955) she was a hilarious caricature feminist who hates men and does not want her niece (Madhubala) to get married. When she has to marry to lay her hands on her fortune, the aunt drags her and the 'fake' husband (Guru Dutt) to court for a divorce. In *Professor* (1962) she played a similarly nutty man-hater who falls in love with Shammi Kapoor disguised as an old man! In *Junglee* (1961) Lalita Pawar was the horrid mother who does not allow her children to smile or laugh. The several cruel mothers-in-law she played were a lark as compared to this role.

In the gangster films of the 1950s, there had to be molls to perform seductive cabaret numbers in sexy clothes that were not allowed to virtuous heroines: they included Geeta Bali in *Baazi* (1951), Shakeela in *Aar Paar* (1952), Sheila Ramani in *Taxi Driver* (1954), Nadira singing the unforgettable *Mud Mud Ke Na Dekh* (Don't turn and stare) in *Shree 420* (1955); and Waheeda Rehman in *CID* (1956). The molls and their Indianized counterparts, the *tawaifs* (courtesans), were usually redeemed by their

Lalita Pawar – the Mother-in-law from hell.

love for the hero and died taking a bullet
meant for him. If there was no scope for a moll,
the narrow-waisted Cuckoo would be brought
in to perform the mandatory dance number.

In *Aan* (1952) Nadira played the imperious
princess dressed in breeches, who is tamed
by the hero (Dilip Kumar) and made to wear
ghaghra cholis (a long traditional costume and
blouse) as a mark of her induction into the fold

Danny Denzongpa with
Nadira in **AASHIQ HOON
BAHARON KA.**

of the good *Bharatiya Nari* (traditional Indian
woman). Various shrews have been tamed
since, right up to Sridevi in *Laadla* (1994)
who acted as a snobbish career-woman, the
equivalent of a 1950s princess. Husn Bano,
Kuldeep Kaur and Manorama plotted and
schemed in dozens of films, but they never
quite matched the sheer cruelty of Surya
Kumari in *Udan Khatola* (1956) or the devious
games of Shyama in *Bhai Bhai* (1956) and
Bhabhi (1956) and *Sharda* (1957). Surya Kumari
also played an evil step-mother in *Milan* (1967),
thus completing the circle of wickedness.

In *Main Nashe Mein Hoon* (1959), Nishi
vowed revenge against a hanging judge
(Mubarak), seduced his son (Raj Kapoor) and
turned him into an alcoholic. Nigar Sultana
played a classy vamp in *Mughal-e-Azam*
(1960) and gave the heroine Madhubala a run
for her money as she vied for attention from
the prince, Dilip Kumar.

Meanwhile Helen took over from Cuckoo
as the 'item' dance girl. The most graceful
and accomplished dancer in Hindi films,
she also occasionally got performing roles.
In the memorable thriller *Teesri Manzil* (1966)
she played the part of a cabaret dancer and
accomplice of the mysterious killer. Again, in

Pagla Kahin Ka (1970), she betrays her boyfriend (Shammi Kapoor) with his best friend (Prem Chopra). Shashikala attempted to play the sophisticated vamp in a blonde wig in *Phool Aur Patthar* (1966) but soon after settled down to regular roles in family socials.

In the 1969 family melodrama, *Do Raaste*, newcomer Bindu played the classic home-breaker – rich girl married into a happy joint family – who starts creating misunderstanding between brothers and, urged on by her mother (Leela Mishra), forces her husband (Prem Chopra) to abandon his family. Padma Khanna's most memorable moments were in *Johny Mera Naam* (1970) where she was forced to do a titillating striptease to save her boyfriend's life, and *Saudagar* (1973), where she played opposite Amitabh Bachchan as a vain and lazy wife. *Caravan* (1971) had Aruna Irani do the best dance numbers, as a gypsy in love with the hero, Jeetendra.

Many dancers played vamps, including Madhumati, Jayshree T, Fariyal and Laxmi Chhaya – but Aruna Irani and Bindu were the most successful of the lot, as they were also good actresses. They were equally adept at Indianized roles and westernized moll roles, could do a *mujra* (dance performed by

a *nautch* girl) or a cabaret number as well as play the conniving home-breaker to perfection. Till as late as *Hum Aapke Hain Kaun* (1994), Bindu was playing a wicked woman who is slapped by her husband and immediately becomes the dutiful wife, for which she is also rewarded with a pregnancy after years of childlessness! In *Beta* (1994), Aruna Irani dextrously played the deceitful step-mother who almost kills her stepson (Anil Kapoor) with kindness.

In Bollywood films, the 'bad' mother is reviled almost as much as the step-mother. Rekha in *Do Anjaane* (1976) and Manisha Koirala in *Akele Hum Akele Tum* (1995) appear to have committed a sin by giving priority to their careers in preference to their children, and Tina Munim in *Sauten* (1984) seems hateful because she does not want children at all!

Really strong negative female characters, as opposed to caricatures, are hard to come by. One exception was Hema Malini's superb role and *tour-de-force* performance in *Lal Patthar* (1971) as the mistress jealous of her man's (Raaj Kumar) wife, Rakhee. Rakhee herself played the evil/good sister in the 'double-role' hit, *Sharmilee* (1977), following in the footsteps

Nanda as killer with Sujit
Kumar in B.R. Chopra's
ITTEFAQ. A murder
mystery without songs.

of Nargis in *Anhonee* (1952) and Nadia in
Muqabla (1942).

There have been few truly vile women in
Hindi films: the adulterous murderer Nanda in
Ittefaq (1969), the man-eating Helen in *Mere
Jeevan Saathi* (1972), Bindu in *Hawas* (Lust),
the sophisticated gold-digging killer Simi in
Karz (1980), Sujata Mehta as the step-mother
eyeing her stepson in *Yateem* (1989), Amrita
Singh in *Aaina* (1993), making a play for the
man she rejected who is now married to her
sister. On the whole, filmmakers have not been
too imaginative in their portrayal of wicked
women.

With the arrival on the scene of the
uninhibited actresses of the 1970s – Zeenat
Aman, Parveen Babi, Reena Roy, Tina Munim
and Kimi Katkar – the cabaret-dancer moll
was made redundant. The heroines were
now the ones who wore skimpy clothes and
performed sexy dance numbers. No vamp
had ever gyrated as seductively as Zeenat
Aman to the *Aap Jaisa Koi* number in *Qurbani*
(1979) or performed *mujras* (dance by
courtesans) as suggestively as Rekha in
Muqaddar Ka Sikander (1978) or as provoca-
tively as Madhuri Dixit to the beat of the *Ek Do
Teen* in *Tezaab* (1988). And which vamp ever

wore clothes as skimpy as those of Karisma
Kapoor, Urmila Matondkar, Raveena Tandon
and the new crop of leading ladies?

Periodically there are films with female
avenging-angels. Good examples are Sujata
Mehta in *Pratighaat* (1987), Rekha in *Khoon
Bhari Maang* (1988), Dimple Kapadia in
Zakhmee Aurat (1998) and Sridevi in *Sherni*
(1999). But as is apparent even from the titles
of the films, these women were just snatching
the justice that has been denied to them
and their characters, therefore, cannot be
considered to be vamps.

An attempt to 'humanize' the avenger or
terrorist was made by Mani Ratnam in *Dil Se*
(1998) and Santosh Sivan in *The Terrorist*
(1998) – both telling essentially the same
story; the former on a multi-crore scale, the

Prem Chopra as the lecherous
villain. Here with Parveen
Babi in SITAMGAR

Sanjay Dutt plays the devil
with Manisha Koirala in
KHAUFF.

Hema Malini and
Shatrughan Sinha dancing
in **PHANSI KE BAAD**.

Amrish Puri in **DHARMA
SANKAT**.

latter on a shoestring budget. The heroines of *Dil Se* (Manisha Koirala) and *The Terrorist* (Ayesha Dharkar) are young women who have joined militant groups in the belief that they will be able to get justice for their brutalized people. However, both films also took the simplistic stand of sympathizing with the terrorist and holding a callous establishment responsible for their condition.

Of the several *Fatal Attraction* rehashes, *Pyar Tune Kya Kiya* (2001) is the most slick. Urmila Matondkar plays a woman so obsessed with Fardeen Khan that she tries to break up his marriage and kill his wife (Sonali Kulkarni). She finally goes mad. She is a female equivalent of Shah Rukh Khan in *Darr*. Kajol in *Gupt* (1997) and Urmila Matondkar in *Kaun* (1999) played mentally deranged killers, but they were unable to really scare the audience.

Even today, the most evil thing a woman can do is break up a home. In *Hum Saath Saath Hain* (1999) the home-breakers were three single women – Kunika, Kalpana Iyer and Jayshree T. They were mockingly called *titlis* (butterflies) who were shown smoking, playing cards in clubs and enticing the good woman, Reema Lagoo, to mistreat her step-son – a throwback to the *Ramayana* where Manthara similarly leads Kaikayi astray. Vamps are rebellious women who do not obey the laws of family supremacy.

The only film character who did as she pleased and was not labelled a loose woman or a vamp was the stunt queen, best personified by Fearless Nadia. The only female character who went beyond the pale and was admired for it was Phoolan Devi in Shekhar Kapur's *Bandit Queen* (1994) – but then she was supposed to be a real character and even the most conservative film tradition cannot argue with reality!

Bollywood: Next Generation

preceding page
LAGAAN
Aamir Khan and Gracy Singh.
A.R. Rahman's music pulsates
in this film which has won
international acclaim.

KAHO NAA PYAAR HAI
Hrithik became the
heart-throb of the nation
after this, his debut film.
And with this film
New Zealand became
Bollywood's new
heaven-on-earth.

Frolicking in the snow has
become a favourite past-
time for Indian actors.

KAHO NAA PYAAR HAI

Hrithik Roshan and Amisha
Patel.

Bollywood never says die. Films fall on their faces like ninepins. Mumbai mafia pop up with their guns, in extortion-mode. Money becomes scarce. Stars play up. Halls run on empty. But like Tom and Jerry, it always zooms back into shape, no matter how battered and bruised. Bollywood men have always talked big. And for a while, the bravado had a hollow ring to it. But, lately, you can hear the buzz again in tinsel town. Something seems to be going right. It may have begun with the desi Hercules, Hrithik Roshan and his amazing ascension to the top early last year with his debut film *Kaho Naa Pyaar Hai* – and good takings at the box-office. However, a drought followed. But with the amazing record-breaking success of *Gadar Ek Prem Katha* and *Lagaan* (2001), life in Bollywood has become beautiful once again.

There's a sense of confidence evident in the films now being made by younger directors. A new breeze is blowing through here, and nowhere is this more evident than in Farhan Akhtar's debut film *Dil Chahta Hai* – a humorous story about three young men who have just graduated from college. Slickly edited, this film carries no baggage of moral posturings, and for once, people in the film talk as they do in real life. One of the heroes is even in love with an older woman – unheard of in Bollywood.

There is a new trend in film locations; today, most of the action seems to be taking place in some never-never land, unrelated to any specific geography or history, or in most cases, any semblance of logic. It is almost as if the new breed of directors has magic carpets to fly off wherever – and whenever – their

**DILWALE DULHANIA LE
JAYENGE**
Shah Rukh Khan, Kajol and
Amrish Puri. This charming
blockbuster, which had
everyone dancing in
the aisles - both in India
and overseas - had a
conservative core. Even in
this New Age of Consent,
Papa still knows best.

whims dictate (almost mid-sentence, as it were). Switzerland has long been a fantasy-land, especially for Yash Chopra's dreamy lovers. It has long been the Indian idea of paradise – the ultimate escape with its pristine mountains, lakes and natural beauty, not to forget its clockwork efficiency. More recently, directors have begun to look beyond Europe. Take two releases of the summer of 2001. In *Ek Rishtaa: Story of a Bond* the young couple, Akshay Kumar and Karisma Kapoor, are suddenly transported from an unidentified city in India, to the pristine beaches of New Zealand. In *Muhje Kuch Kehna Hai* the young lovers Kareena Kapoor and Tusshar Kapoor, also suddenly surface in New Zealand. Ever since the amazing success of Rakesh Roshan's *Kaho Na Pyaar Hai* (2000) – and the almost instant canonization of its debuting hunk-hero, Hrithik Roshan – New Zealand seems the Next Best Thing for directors.

Neither of the couples had actually left Indian shores. Nor indeed have the countless young lovers and their huge joint families in many of the Hindi films now being made. The environs of a picturesque Rajasthani *haveli* (mansion) or village are likely to have nothing to do with the land of the Rajputs - the

beautiful hills and lush green rolling country-side could be Bohemia or even Scotland. But then, the imagination needs no passport. The new pattern of filmmaking is conceived here but not necessarily all made-in-India. Says veteran screenwriter Suraj Sanim: 'Each film unit goes abroad and invariably shoots songs, but since last year it has become a natural feature. Even if the story is taking place in Chamba, Subash Ghai will go to Toronto.'

Just as Hollywood inspired the Italians to recreate America in Europe for the spaghetti westerns of the 1970s, so Bollywood is recreating India abroad: we are now beginning to see the 'Burger Eastern'. The new breed of globetrotting directors now do their location shooting just about anywhere abroad, from beautiful Budapest to the lush green rolling countryside of Scotland.

In its post-liberalization, post-branding age, India is looking more like a mini-Europe or United States. People drink Pepsi, eat at McDonalds, wear Tommy Hilfiger, Gap or Armani (even if they are poor). They live in out-of-Manhattan lofts and their children go to schools which appear to have materialized out of Beverly Hills. The yuppy Mumbai police station in a recent film, *One Two Ka Four*

opposite

YAADEIN

Hrithik Roshan in Subash

Ghai's most hyped film.

(2001), makes the *NYPD Blue* offices look like the slums of Bombay's Dharavi on a bad day.

This is a strange hybrid cinema. For, while the stories may be situated in a no-man's land with characters who often look and sound as if they have walked off the sets of American B-movies or TV soaps, the core of the film is still Indian. In fact, it could not be more traditional. The family is always sacred and so are the country and its traditions. In the 1990s there was a flurry of films with songs and dialogues that were paeans to India and Indian traditions. In Aditya Chopra's *Dilwale Dulhania le Jayenge* (1995), the slick young NRI (Non-Resident Indian) hero refuses to elope with his beloved. He insists on her family accepting him. And Subash Ghai's *Pardes* had the audience on its feet with the number '*Yeh Mera India*' (This is my India). The film itself pitched the traditional Indian against his more corrupt avtaar in the West – the ubiquitous NRI (Non-Resident Indian). Patriotism and a fair amount of jingoism are now creeping into many films.

However, it is not just a question of a *desi dil* (Indian heart) being slickly packaged with state-of-the-art technology. There is also an affirmation of traditional and often regressive

MAINE PYAR KIYA

Salman Khan and

Bhagyashree.

A landmark film which

brought back romance to

Bollywood after a long spell

of action films. It also

spelled the return of melody

to Hindi film songs and the

triumph of family values

and, of course, love.

values. This major shift is largely the work of three young directors, Sooraj Barjatya, Aditya Chopra and Karan Johar. This triumvirate has cast the longest shadows over popular Hindi films during the last decade. They have brought in a New Age of Bollywood by combining western gloss with Indian soul. We have fusion cinema to go with fusion music, and fusion food.

In 1989 Barjatya, the leader of this brat pack, then in his mid-twenties, brought back the age of romance and melody with his debut film *Maine Pyar Kiya*. This sweet musical brought the Indian Joint Family back into the picture – back to the fore, to be precise. There was a temporary respite from violence.

And thus was born the age of squeaky-clean cinema, of life filmed through rose-tinted glasses in which most things were sweetness and light. More important, the audiences began to flock into the cinema houses again.

Until then, Bollywood had been in limbo. By the mid-1980s Amitabh Bachchan was no longer able to play the angry young man persona that launched a thousand clones. The protagonists of these action films were urban loners; the family practically disappeared, at the very most being represented by a widowed mother. Many films were no more than cinematic collages of videos of Hollywood movies such as *Dirty Harry* and *Scarface*. Good and evil were played out with stereotypes – white hats pitted against black hats. The demon-killing hero formula from the ancient Indian epics fitted like a dream into the revenge sagas inspired by American films.

The era of Manmohan Desai and his inimitable school of variety entertainment filmmaking had also peaked by the mid-1980s. By then, Prakash Mehra, Ramesh Sippy and Hrishikesh Mukherjee had made their most important works. Subhash Ghai had also made his mark in the Bollywood dream machine with films like *Ram Lakhan* (1989) and *Saudagar* (1991).

Later directors, fed on a diet of Hollywood, introduced a certain technical savvy and slickness into commercial films. Mani Ratnam and Ram Gopal Varma, both from South India, made more use of the grammar of western cinema. With *Roja* (1994), *Bombay* (1995) and *Dil Se* (1998), Ratnam brought news headlines and what was behind them into popular cinema. His films were rooted in real life, albeit a romanticized one, with fairly large doses of melodrama and pop patriotism. These films were set in a context and tackled such taboo subjects as communalism and casteism. Later, Santosh Sivan even tried to explore the mind of a militant in *Terrorist* (1997).

Varma's particular contribution was fancy camera work and stylized photography. His briskly edited *Rangeela*, (1995) pulsated with the daring energy of western music videos. MTV had reached Bollywood shores, and with *Satya*, (1998) he delivered a gritty, gut-wrenching portrayal of the Mumbai underbelly and underworld. *Satya* looked like a Hollywood product with Indian characters, settings and story. And for a while in the 1990s, both family and action films dominated the film scene with actors like Sunny Deol,

HUM AAPKE HAIN KAUN
Salman Khan and Madhuri Dixit. Love, sacrifice and family are the key words in this long musical saga in which all's well that ends well.

HUM DIL DE CHUKE SANAM
Salman Khan and Aishwarya Rai. A lavishly shot love story with sylvan Hungarian countryside standing in for village-India.

preceding page

DILWALE DULHANIA LE JAYENGE

Kajol and Shah Rukh Khan. Spontaneity and verve mark the performances of the two actors who serve up screen magic. It elevated both to new age superstars.

right

KUCH KUCH HOTA HAI

Kajol and Shah Rukh Khan. One of the biggest hits ever, this debut film by Karan Johar, one of India's youngest directors. Western gloss clothed Indian soul and the film's refrain: friends can be lovers.

Akshay Kumar and Sunil Shetty.

But these films were mainly successful in metropolitan cities: they failed to set the entire nation on fire. Bollywood had to wait for Barjatya to tap into the collective psyche, to capture the hearts of grannies, teenyboppers and overseas Indians alike – and to come up with a money-spinning formula for success.

Maine Pyar Kiya was the film that broke records and made its director the new Midas of the celluloid world. It also started a trend for long titles that sound like lines from a song

and are invariably abbreviated to their initials. Barjatya's two films, *Hum Aapke Hain Kaun - HAHK* (1994) and *Hum Saath Saath Hain – HSSH* (1999) continued the winning streak. Following the same formula and achieving some of the same appeal, were Aditya Chopra's *Dilwale Dulhania Le Jayenge – DDLJ* (1995), Karan Johar's *Kuch Kuch Hota Hai – KKHH* (1998) and Sanjay Leela Bhansali's *Hum Dil De Chuke Sanam – HDDCS* (1999).

This new generation of under-thirties had its finger on the nation's pulse. Though they

DIL TO PAGAL HAI
Karisma Kapoor and
Madhuri Dixit. Yash
Chopra's ode to love, hit a
chord with the youth, with
his theme of *'someone,
somewhere is made for you'*.

had grown up with Hollywood, then readily
available on satellite TV and Indian cinemas,
they were firmly rooted in Bollywood, and
Indian traditions. 'It's an old mind in a new
body', says director Mahesh Bhatt, whose
own films – especially *Ashiqui* (1990) and *Dil
Hai Ke Manta Nahin* (1991) won considerable
success in the 1990s. Bhatt attributes the
unprecedented rise of this new tribe of
cineastes to 'packaging, which just got better
and better, and to glitter'. Not to forget the
Indian heart, beating beneath all the glitzy
trappings.

Take *Kuch Kuch Hota Hai (KKHH)*,
Johar's three-hour-long epistle to love. Rani
Mukherjee plays the heroine, newly returned
from Oxford. She dresses in sports shorts,
tube tops and shimmering minis that hug
her Apsara-like curves. But, on cue, when
challenged to sing by her college-mates, she
breaks into a perfect, soul-tingling *Om Jai
Jagdish Hare* (Praised be the Lord) – and the
audience claps, ecstatic. The gods are in their
heaven and all's well with the world: the
winds of the West have not blown through
Indian *pooja* rooms. These young filmmakers
neither needed to look too hard nor too far, to
understand that there had been a significant

generational shift in the attitude of today's
youth towards religion and the family.

They just looked around them. On any
given Thursday, young women in lycra Capri
pants and young men with ear studs and
ponytails, fill the Shirdi Baba temples in India.
On any Tuesday, over ninety per cent of the
people in serpentine queues outside the
Hanuman *mandirs* (temples), are under
thirty. Fasts have become *de rigeur* amongst
young people across all religions: more
and more youngsters are now fasting during
Lent, *Ramzan* or *Navaratras*. (Ironically, the
parents of this generation may not have
been the fasting kind.) And calendar gods
increasingly adorn computers in many
high-tech offices. Like their NRI counterparts,
yuppies whizzing past in Santros and Ford
Ikons have *bhajans* (Hindu religious songs)
blaring from their stereo car radios as they
drive to work. Rituals and rites make the new
economy easier to digest.

The new generation of directors under-
stands that you now need to have paeans both
to the gods and to the family. Barjatya's trilogy
was just that: an ode to the Indian joint family
and *status quo*. He was tapping the nostalgia
for a more hermetic, safer world, where you

Posters of
MAINE PYAR KIYA and
**DILWALE DULHANIA
LE JAYENGE.**

can eat nice things all day, sing and wear silk
saris. His formula, which others later followed,
was simple: the family became an enclave,
protected by the tall doors of their sprawling
mansion.

From *Maine Pyar Kiya* to *Hum Aapke Hain
Kaun* and *Hum Saath Saath Hain*, the outside
world impinges less and less. Wars may rage,
poverty spread and politicians might continue
to manipulate the people, but nothing filters
through. Nothing really exists outside the clan.
As filmmaker Shyam Benegal observes: 'Today
it is the story – the family, the Indian family
and its traditions, which defines the film – and
you can take this and set it down anywhere.'

The Barjatya family has aunts, uncles,
friends-who-have-become-family, dogs and
servants-as-family who comprise a universe
unto themselves. Sociologist Patricia Uberoi
describes *Hum Aapke Hain Kaun (HAHK)* 'as
the story of the Indian family as a form of
"imagined community"… the family as an icon
of the national society'. This is the family, not
as it is, but as it *should* be.

And the family comes first. In fact, the back
of the white jeep owned by Prem (Salman
Khan), the main protagonist of *HAHK*, has the
words: *I love my family,* next to its number-

plates. He is also 'prepared to sacrifice his
individual love for the sake of his family'. The
woman he loves (Madhuri Dixit) is supposed
to marry Salman's elder brother, her dead
sister's husband, in order to look after their
child. The director's third film, *HSSH* is a
modern-day *Ramayana,* centred round
sacrifice and filial duty. Like Lakshman and
Bharat, the brothers refuse to sit on the chair
of the adopted son when their mother throws
him out.

The fact that romantic love is subservient
to larger interests of the family, is also
apparent in both Chopra's *DDLJ* and
Bhansali's *HDDCS,* as well as in the works of
other lesser known Barjatya wannabes. The
young female protagonist of Chopra's first
film – an effervescent and sprightly Kajol – is
willing to elope with her NRI lover, but he
is unwilling to marry without the blessings
of her stern father. Apparently, Chopra's
father, the creator of gossamer romances
(the enduring *Kabhi Kabhie, Lamhe* (1989)
and *Chandni* (1989)) challenged the logic of
his son's conservative stance. But his son
obviously had a better idea of what his generation was all about: parental blessings are a
must. In Karan Johar's forthcoming star-studded

Aishwarya Rai. A Miss World turned model and actress who has achieved star status in Bollywood today.

Preity Zinta. Effervescent and cute, Zinta who was first spotted by Director Shekhar Kapur has all the attributes of the girl-next-door, she also brings attitude to the screen.

film (Amitabh Bachchan, Shah Rukh Khan, Hrithik Roshan, Jaya Bachchan and Kareena Kapoor) shot mostly in the UK, the family and parents acquire an even brighter halo. Similarly, in Bhansali's film, an equally vivacious Aishwarya Rai marries the man her parents choose for her, though she loves someone else. And this in the year 2000!

In this new school of filmmaking, the look of a film is all-important. The 1990s saw the emergence of a crop of young writers, musicians, choreographers, art directors, fashion designers, stylists, distributors, make-up men and publicists who could whip up sleek, good-looking films with airbrushed protagonists. They no longer needed to rely on tired, pirated videos of American movies for inspiration.

Suddenly, the third world began to look very much like the first world. 'There was an obsession with looks – all had a homogeneous look, as if they had come out of some kind of assembly line', says Mahesh Bhatt. The Bollywood dream factory churned out standard-issue creatures: actresses looked like catwalk models and actors emerged prefabricated with pop-up muscles and baby faces, all of them identical. Business boomed

for cosmetic surgeons and dentists. The gyms of Mumbai began to overflow.

The 1990s was also the decade that Indian women began to win Miss World and Miss Universe crowns with uncanny regularity – almost as if by right of birth. Beauty Queens extended their reign to Bollywood: the picture-perfect former Miss World Aishwarya Rai has won an exalted position in the celluloid pantheon. Sushmita Sen, the saucier former Miss Universe, is also a rising star – as are other beauty queens and models including Mahima Choudhury and Preity Zinta. Nor should we forget the men: Arjun Ramphal, Dino Morea and Milind Soman crossed over from the catwalk – and now Mr India, Aryan Vaid, is all set to flex his histrionic muscles.

Yash Chopra is the Godfather of the good-looking musical, spun around wedding rituals and young lovers canoodling in picturesque Switzerland or in a castle-dotted quaint English countryside. The next generation, including his son Aditya, reworked these 'champagne-and-chiffon' musical sagas, giving them a modern, technically savvy and upbeat look. But while they borrowed much from Yash Chopra, they forgot one essential element – the strong story-line. The plots are

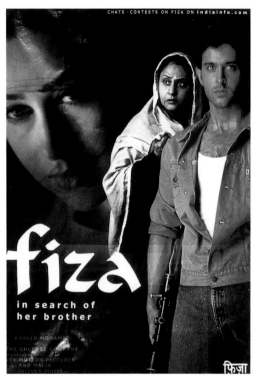

wafer-thin, squeezed by an obsessive pursuit
of technical excellence.

Barjatya jump-started another Bollywood
trend: musical romances in which the
narrative is reduced to interludes in a string of
song-and-dance numbers. *HAHK* has fourteen
songs, two weddings and a funeral. Aditya
Chopra's second venture, *Mohabattein* (2001)
is four hours of musical numbers. Lamenting
this trend, director Rajiv Menon has said in a
recent interview that content is disappearing
from most of the films being made. 'There
is a total absence of conflict in the hero, there
is love, a marriage, happiness, a bridal
sequence, a small misunderstanding, and the
happiness again. It is frightening.'

Bollywood is churning out feel-good,
peppy, popcorn romances. Energy is the key

word – the new currency. (Think of the Bar-
One chocolate advertisement which exhorts
you to 'get more out of life'.) And even the
seasoned Yash Chopra succumbed to this new
film credo in his latest film *Dil To Pagal Hai*
(2000) – another soft-focus romantic film with
beautiful people (Madhuri Dixit, Shah Rukh
Khan and Karisma Kapoor) singing one lovely
and beautifully choreographed song after
another. Only love matters to the characters of
this quintessential escapist film. There is no
context for the action, no outside world here to
speak off. Instead you have an insulated
universe, a self-conscious world of Archie
comics. And who needs the real-life problems
of corruption, when you can have stars,
snow-capped alpine peaks and of course,
tons of romance.

A scene from **YAADEIN**
Subhash Ghai's tale about
friendship between a father
and his three daughters.

DHAI AKSHAR PREM KE

A walk in the clouds for Abhishek Bachchan and Aishwarya Rai.

MUJHE KUCCH KEHNA HAI

Kareena Kapoor and Tusshaar Kapoor. A surprise hit movie about a tongue-tied young man.

Scenes from **HUM AAPKE HAIN KAUN** (top) and **AA AB LAUT CHALE**

Chopra Senior may have introduced north Indian and Aryanized wedding rituals into Bollywood, but it was Barjatya who took these devices to their extreme. He used them all – and more. Uberoi writes: 'In the unfolding of the story of *HAHK,* a series of important rites of passage – betrothal, engagement, the *mehndi* (the bride's hands and feet are decorated with henna), and marriage ceremonies, a seventh month pregnancy ritual, and celebrations of childbirth (including the visit of the *hijras (*eunuchs) to bless the newborn child) are all presented in their non-Sanskritic idioms.' She then adds that the wedding ceremony itself is 'no more than a suggestive backdrop for the enactment of "teasing" of the young men of the groom's party by the bride's sisters and friends'. The wedding-video school of moviemaking had arrived. Barjatya spared us none of the rites and rituals associated with pregnancy and childbearing. The same was true of Bhansali with *HDDCS*. And, of course, each ritual called for a song.

Bollywood films became more and more like Broadway musicals. Filmmakers became entertainers. The return of romance brought the return of music. Until the late 1980s, action

movies dominated: Salim-Javed authored films did not need music, they depended on dialogue. Mahesh Bhatt believes that his own film *Ashiqui* sparked the musical trend. 'Music companies got into the act of producing films in the 1990s. They felt that since they had the hardware, they could also produce the software… In fact, the late Gulshan Kumar [audio-cassette baron and owner of T series] has an important role in all this – *Ashiqui* was the *HAHK* of the music world.' The boom in the audio world was vital: the film industry had been losing out to video piracy. Music became a basic territory.

Music companies such as Venus and Tips became film production companies, changing not only the content of films but also the way they were made. Marketing became a major concern. To push the music, the companies began to make films with audios called shorts. As Mahesh Bhatt describes it: 'For these promos you needed good-looking products, just as you needed good-looking young people to sell Coke, you needed the kind of stars who could seduce you to buy the music.' Next came film trailers and the songs aired while the film was still in production. Soon music was reverberating from everywhere: from cars on

1942: A LOVE STORY
Manisha Koirala, Anil
Kapoor and Jackie Shroff.
Shroff as a young
revolutionary steals the
show despite his brief
appearance in the film.
The music is incredibly
good and the song
sequences reveal Raj
Kapoor as the muse.

the street, wedding halls, countless song-based film shows on television, FM radios and disco floors. Satellite television became the great equalizer: even snobs who professed not to like Hindi film music, found themselves dancing to Hindi film hits in discos and night-clubs. MTV gave legitimacy to *filmi* pop. And when Gulshan Kumar slashed the price of audiocassettes to Rs. 25 and increased payments to singers, everybody including film producers, started dancing to the tune of the music companies.

Music composers were now paid as much as the stars. Songs became the best advertise-ments for films. For *1942: A Love Story,* director Vidhu Vinod Chopra hired 'a special director [Sanjay Leela Bhansali] for songs'.

The day of the mega song had arrived. Producers thought about the songs even before the filming began. Directors began to spend as much as half their budget just on the songs. Director Padam Kumar spent Rs. 1.5. crore for just one song in his film, *Indian.* It was back to the future, with fresh attempts to emulate the grandeur of classics such as *Mughal-e-Azam (*1960*)* or *Pakeezah* (1971).

Latter-day Cecil B. de Milles flourished. Big became beautiful: Indian film directors could now summon up any era, from any corner of the earth. They became masters of illusion. Eclectic was the key word. For his film, *Josh,* Mansoor Khan had over 736 men work for over a month to create Vasco, a Goan town with a 125-foot high church and tall coconut trees. For *Indian,* Padam Kumar conjured the Colosseum, Spanish Steps, and structures from the ancient city of Harappa. Nearly 500 workers toiled for over thirty days to build the five-storey high Gujarati *haveli* through which the singing Aishwarya flits like a motorized swan in *HDDCS.* Bhansali has gone many steps further with his next film, a remake of *Devdas* (1935; 1955): a sprawling palace has emerged in Mumbai's Film City. Here, in this palace which cost Rs 11 crore, Shah Rukh and Madhuri Dixit will play out the eternal love story.

Meanwhile, the grip of the dynasties of the film industry also loosened. The Chopras, Johars and Barjatyas found they had company in Bollywood. Tanuja Chandra is that rare thing in commercial Hindi film – a woman director. To date she has made two films, *Dushman* (1998) and *Sanghursh* (1999). She is optimistic: 'You no longer have just the studio system, or the Kapoor Khandan, or the Chopra Khandan. Anybody can come in.'

Posters of **PAKEEZAH** and **DUSHMAN**

PYAR TUNE KYA KIYA

Urmila Matondkar and
Fardeen Khan. Fatal
Attraction gets an Indian
avtar in this tale of
obsessive love.

PAAGALPAN

Karan Nath and Aarti.

Amitabh Bachchan in a
scene from **AKS**. Although
the film did not do well it
was a brave attempt at
trying out new genres.

opposite page
MOHRA

Raveena Tandon and
Akshay Kumar. The sizzling
Mast Mast number by the
lead pair made Raveena
into an oomph girl and
Akshay's hip-swiveling
won him many fans.

The television boom of the 1990s opened
the door to Bollywood for many young filmmakers. Tanuja Chandra herself started with
television in 1993: 'Everybody in the country
was making a TV serial, including the local
*paanwallah (*paan seller) and the director's
driver. Lots of people came in from television.
The film industry had become incestuous,
insular and the same old thing. Now there are
attempts to experiment.' Later, journalists
started flocking in. Khalid Mohamed, editor of
Filmfare, made quite an entrée into Bollywood
with *Fiza* (2000), while television journalist
Kunal Kohli has launched his Bollywood career
with *Mujhse Dosti Karoge.*

1999 alone saw as many as fourteen new
directors in Bollywood. They included Mahesh
Manjrekar and Sanjay Chhel, as well as the
Ram Gopal Varma protégé, E. Niwas, who
made *Shool* (1999), remarkable for its critically
acclaimed portrayal of Mumbai's underbelly.

The newest players in Bollywood came
mainly from the world of advertising and
music, seduced perhaps by the critical and
commercial success of ad-man John Mathew
Matthan's *Sarfarosh,* a crisp and gritty
portrayal of cross-border terrorism. It has
powerhouse performances from Aamir Khan
and Naseeruddin Shah. Rajat Mukherjee, yet
another protégé of Varma, has already made
an impact with *Pyar Tune Kya Kiy*a. (2001).
Veteran ad filmmaker Kailashnath
Surendranath is making *Love You Hamesha.*
Rakesh Mehra is another ad-man who has
found the lure of tinsel town irresistible. His
slick music video and ads impressed Amitabh
Bachchan who is now acting in two or three of
his films including *Aks* (2001), a different kind
of thriller which questions the way we look at
good and evil.

A strange new breeze of optimism is
blowing through the city by the Arabian Sea.
'I feel that the wheel is turning, the disillusionment is over. People are more pragmatic, they
are trying things', says Rakesh Mehra, who
believes that India is on its way to becoming a
global player. This confidence to experiment,
which is drawing in hopefuls from varied
backgrounds, springs from the fact that there
is now room for different kinds of cinema.

The future of Indian cinema points to
diversity: a smorgasbord of films with something for everybody. Newcomer Mahesh
Manjrekar made a modest, sensitive film
*Astitva (*2000) about infidelity that became a
talking point in middle-class drawing rooms.

Rajiv Menon had a runaway success with his delightful *Kandukondain, Kandukondain*, a Tamil take on Jane Austen's novel *Sense and Sensibility.* The small film had subtitles, and subtitled films had long been restricted to the art house and festival circuits. Moreover, the subtitled version of the Italian film, *Life is Beautiful* by Roberto Benigni, did surprisingly well. Both young Aditya Chopra's *Mohabbatein* (2001*)* – a sleekly packaged, star-studded musical extravaganza – as well as sexagenarian Shyam Benegal's elegantly made period love story *Zubeidaa* (2001) have been box-office successes in the new millennium, especially outside India. Obviously, something had changed: is it the tastes of the audience, or are there now different kinds of audiences going to the movies? The answer is probably both.

It is the emergence in the big cities of the multiplexes that seems to have the greatest impact on the landscape of Indian cinema. The multiplexes are already providing a platform for different kinds of films. Along with satellite television, they have changed the economics of film distributors. Small movies and experimental films now have a chance of survival. Delhi already has a couple of cinema multiplexes, and more are mushrooming. Mumbai will soon have a new complex with five screens, one of which will be reserved exclusively for offbeat films. Others are being planned in Ahmedabad, Pune, Delhi and Mumbai.

Filmmakers have caught on to the fact that productions with small or middling budgets are the new order of the day. The various new platforms mean that cheaper films will be able to find distributors more readily, and they in turn will be able to recover their costs more quickly. This way, even a moderately successful film will make enough money to qualify as a hit, and producers will get another chance. Filmmakers need to make more intimate films, tailored to auditoriums seating 200 or 300 people, rather than to gargantuan theatres with over 2000 seats.

It has increasingly become a question of pricing. Following underworld financing scandals, provoked by the arrest of the financier and entertainment tycoon, Bharat Shah, there has been a downsizing. 'Play safe' is the current mantra at companies such as Sony and Universal. Tanuja Chandra says 'My budget is now Rs. 3 crore. If it is a hit, you have money on the table, I have understood that

RAM JAANE

Shah Rukh Khan and Juhi
Chawla in a film directed
by Rajiv Mehra.

above right

Abhishek Bachchan. The
son of Amitabh Bachchan,
he has yet to make his mark
on the Bollywood scene.

now …if you keep your costs low you will get
the next chance to make an experimental film',
she says. Chandra won't be chasing the big
stars for a while.

The pan-Indian film has almost become
extinct. Contemporary blockbusters such as
HAHK or *KKHH* are rare events. We seem to
be entering the age of niche filmmaking –
akin to niche marketing for print and media
advertising. *Ghulam* (1998) was a hit in
Maharashtra, less so in the rest of India and
went unnoticed overseas. *Jaanwar* (1999) and
films similar to it, flopped in the cities and did
well in North India, *Kurukshetra* clicked in
Mumbai, *Fiza* (2000) in Mumbai and Nizam.
Shah Rukh Khan's popularity base is in the
cities and abroad. After Amitabh Bachchan,
Hrithik Roshan is perhaps the only star whose
popularity spans the nation. *Dil Se* flopped in
India but broke records overseas. Subhash

Ghai's film *Taal* – promoted enthusiastically in
the US, with advertising on television, radio
and even the internet – was the first Hindi film
to enter the US Top 20. But it did not cause any
stampedes in India. No wonder filmmakers
with deep pockets are now making films
intended specifically to appeal to the NRI
viewer.

Aamir Khan's *Lagaan,* (2001) a period film
set during the Raj in a small desert village
with an Indo-British cast and a cricket match
at its emotional core, has not only hit the
jackpot, it has been amazingly successful
elsewhere, making the it to UK Top 20. The
box-office success of this film as well as *Gadar*
(2001) has given the depressed film industry
a shot in the arm.

The dramatic growth of the Indian
diaspora market has given Hindi cinema
a fresh lease of life and in the process, has

YASH JOHAR PRESENTS DHARMA PRODUCTION'S

Kabhi Khushi
Kabhie Gham...

"Its all about loving your parents"   KARAN JOHAR

YASH JOHAR PRESENTS DHARMA PRODUCTIONS "KABHI KHUSHI KABHIE GHAM" A KARAN JOHAR FILM
AMITABH BACHCHAN • JAYA BACHCHAN • SHAHRUKH KHAN • KAJOL • HRITHIK ROSHAN SP. APPEARANCE RANI MUKHERJEE
MUSIC JATIN LALIT & SANDESH SHANDILYA GUEST COMPOSER AADESH SRIVASTVA LYRICIST SAMEER ASSOCIATE PRODUCER HIROO JOHAR
ASSOCIATE DIRECTOR NIKHIL ADVANI DIRECTOR OF PHOTOGRAPHY KIRAN DEOHANS PRODUCER YASH JOHAR DIRECTOR KARAN JOHAR

KABHI KHUSI KHABI GHAM.....)
Amitabh Bachchan, Jaya Bachchan,
Shah Rukh Khan, Kajol. Hrithik Roshan
and Kareena Kapoor in Karan Johar's
latest film, which has become an
international success.

NAYAK

Anil Kapoor in a film that was promoted on a grand scale, but has yet to collect revenues at the box-office.

changed the calculations of film distributors. Traditionally, there have been six 'territories' (or areas of film distribution): five in India, and one outside the country. The overseas market used to be looked upon as an afterthought; today it accounts for a major portion of Bollywood earnings – at times as much as forty per cent. This is entirely understandable when you realize that there are about sixty theatres in the United States, and quite a few in the UK. Premieres of films are often held simultaneously in India and abroad. Bollywood promos now go everywhere with satellite television, increasing the awareness of Indian films worldwide. It is now obviously the turn to woo the East as well. Not only have southern star Rajnikanth's Tamil film won over the Japanese (Japanese tourists in buses stop by his house in Chennai as if he were some living monument), Shah Rukh Khan's new period film *Ashoka* (directed by Santosh Sivan) is being premiered in Tokyo. It was also screened at the Venice Film Festival.

The tastes of the international Indian audience have clearly had an impact on Bollywood, determining the choice of the stars, stories and music of film. The NRIs usually want their films to be both trendy and traditional. Above all, they want them to look good and be slickly made. There are candyfloss romances for the second generation, with stars like Shah Rukh Khan, Hrithik Roshan or Karisma Kapoor, and nostalgia-imbued films for the previous one – the Yash Chopra school of gossamer romance revisited and updated. Neither generation wants anything too dark or grim or realistic. And both want reams of music. 'They want their *rajma* – their taste buds expressed through their music. You can see these NRIs in Canada with Indian gods on their dashboards, and the latest Hindi movie songs blaring while they drive. We were catering to that market during the slump. And they have a good-looking film obsession', says Mahesh Bhatt.

Overseas is the new Eldorado for Indian producers. Most of the films now have at least one NRI character – a young Indian coming home in search of his roots or to do research is currently the flavour of the month. Aditya Chopra started the trend with *DDLJ,* featuring Shah Rukh Khan as an NRI who falls in love with Kajol. The feisty single girl is enjoying her last spell of freedom in Europe before she returns home to an arranged marriage. But in fact, Papa Chopra gets there first: the Anil

YAADEIN

Kareena Kapoor and Hrithik Roshan. Most notable about this film is the unmistakable chemistry between the lead pair, in Subhash Ghai's tale.

HUM DIL DE CHUKE SANAM

Aishwarya Rai and Ajay Devgan
in this film that was one of the
biggest hits of 1999.

Kapoor persona in *Lamhe* (1991) lives in England – and of course he too falls in love with a girl from an Indian village.

Initially, there were a few token NRI characters because many films were being made abroad: the foreign locations provided good picturesque backdrops and, later on, greater security, when the Mumbai mafia began to target producers and stars. These days NRIs have moved centre-stage – one example is Hrithik Roshan in *Kaho Naa Pyaar Hai.* Another is Salman Khan in *Hum Dil De Chuke Sanam*, who lives in Italy. More lately, in some sort of role-reversal, you have confident young Kareena Kapoor in *Mujhe Kuch Kehna Hai,* playing an NRI researcher who comes home to India and falls for a shy *desi.*

'Films are reflecting the confusion of a society in transition. The new aspirational model is the NRI who has succeeded in terms of material wealth but still wants to hold on to his Indian values', says film director Govind Nihalani. Like most Indians, the NRI wants the best of both worlds. Both *bhajans* and pop.

Interestingly, the gap between NRIs and those living in India is closing, made narrower by satellite television, Indian television and liberalization. 'There has been a fundamental shift in the way Indians think: during the last three decades they have been exposed to so much more, satellite television, the internet. You now have disposable incomes, sex before marriage, nuclear family and drugs', says distributor Shravan Shroff. Indian soaps paint a very different picture from the one generally observed on the big screen. Moreover, television has raised the general expectations of Indians. N. Chandra says: 'Television has made us all addicted to quick-pace. It grabs you immediately with its hook, its production values. The attention span has been reduced, with an MTV-style cutting of songs.'

There is also a whiff of professionalism in Bollywood. The men in white patent-leather sandals and *paan*-stained teeth are rapidly giving way to the young preppies with MBAs who are well versed in corporate-speak and want to impose a measure of discipline. The twentysomething Shroff, who is now turning producer as well, has hired the same business consultancy firm that advises McDonalds in India. 'You have to marry technology and finance with a sense of the medium', he says.

Production methods may also change with the banks now willing to finance film production. The IDBI bank has offered

above and below

CHAL MERE BHAI

Salman Khan, Sanjay Dutt
and Karisma Kapoor in
this film directed by
David Dhawan.

PARDES

Shah Rukh Khan in Subash
Ghai's love story.

Bollywood directors are
increasingly choosing to
film internationally, because
the cast can be hired for a
month at a time, the movie
can be shot within a much
shorter time frame.

producers Rs. 5 crore for each film. There are, however, many riders to these loans. Perhaps inspired by Steven Spielberg, many directors and indeed some actors, are taking the mantle of producer. Actors Anupam Kher, Aamir Khan, Shah Rukh Khan, Juhi Chawla, Jackie Shroff and Pooja Bhatt have all established production companies. Amitabh Bachchan was the first to do so with ABCL (Amitabh Bachchan Corporation Limited) – which did not quite take off. 'Today the director has to be the producer as well…', says Rakesh Mehra, who undertook both roles in his debut film *Aks,* 'otherwise you have to wait like Shekhar Kapur. We are here not to wait but to make movies.'

Directors like Mehra, whose background is in advertising, do not believe in leaving things to chance: 'I won't sign an actor and pray for his dates. We want to be more professional now. The whole corporate structure is creeping in … time and money become important.'

There are also sporadic attempts by certain groups to change the nature of the films being made. Recently, Manmohan Shetty of Adlabs and owner of the new Imax cinema in Mumbai, brought together directors Govind

Nihalani, Romesh Sharma, Prakash Jha, Pravin Nischol and John Mathew Mattan to form a company. Their brief: to pool their creative and technical resources to produce high-quality films and television software. Earlier Mani Ratnam, Shekhar Kapur and Ram Gopal Varma had started the company, India Talkies, to do just that. They needed to.

Unfortunately, many of the films being churned out by the Bollywood machine are just well packaged fluff, devoid of any real content. The production values may have improved, but good scripts remain the exception. Veteran screenwriter Suraj Sanim who has written *Gadar: Ek Prem Katha* (2001), a love story which unfolds during the Partition of India, says: 'Right from the day I came, the industry was adapting Hollywood or regional hits. They need only dialogue writers. The scriptwriter can be the producer, his wife and occasionally his driver.'

Kamlesh Pandey, who has come to Bollywood from the world of television and advertising, is equally cynical. 'Scripts are still not given any importance. Actors can't read. The only book they read is a chequebook. Many directors may have come from the world of advertising, but you need drama. You have

to have the grammar of mainstream cinema.'

Nevertheless, the possibility of making
digital movies provides some reason for
optimism. The recent international festival of
digital movies organized by Digital Talkies, a
new company with Shekhar Kapur on board,
revealed that there are many bright young
people who desperately want to make movies,
and can now do so, thanks to radically cheaper
and more democratic new technology. 'Scripts
are just pouring in', says Digital Talkies' CEO,
Pia Singh. The company has already made two
feature films.

The time may be ripe for independent
filmmakers. Dev Benegal's *English August*
and *Split Wide Open* (2000), Kaizad Gustad's
Bombay Boys, Nagesh Kukunoor's *Hyderabad
Blues* and *Rockford* (1999) reflect an *auteur's*
voice.

Such films indicate that many of our
younger cineastes are moving beyond making
lazy copies of Hollywood. There is a new
kind of confidence that stems from the
achievements of Indians abroad. But not just
from the success stories of Shekhar Kapur and
Night Shyamalan – nor even Santosh Sivan,
whose film *Terrorist* (1997) made it to the
Sundance Film Festival. It is the amazing

success of the NRIs of Silicon Valley and New
York's Silicon Alley that is the source of much
of this burgeoning self-confidence and can-do
mantra. Rakesh Mehra says: 'I think we are
moving towards a more global subject. We are
changing the whole structure of our society.
We are being accepted as part of the world.
Finally, the stereotypical image of an India of
elephants and maharajas is giving way to
techies. No longer is it just the once-upon-a-
time story. We can't live with the past, we can
tell the stories of the India of today.'

Tell it like it is may well be the new motto
for the latest breed of directors who are
technically savvy, possess degrees from
American and British universities and have
cut their teeth on Hollywood and MTV. With
the pan-Indian film finally buried, cineastes
like Farhan Akhtar, E. Niwas, Anubhav Sinha
and Rohan Sippy can now make films for
specific strata of society. Akhtar's film *Dil
Chahta Hai* (2001), a breezy, humour-filled
and slick story about friendship of three young
men, has broken through the stereotype-
barrier and is still charming young and old
urbanites. They no longer need to make films
that have something for everybody. For
example, *Tum Bin* (2001) has unexpectedly

Karisma Kapoor and
Akshey Kumar

done very well at the box-office in India. The
film is a simple love story about yuppie youth.
The debutant director (Sinha is a music video
director and adman) cast models to play the
main characters in his film. Another filmmaker
to be watched is Meghna Gulzar, whose
debut film *Filhaal* is about friendship, love
and the unpredictability of life. Trained in film
production in New York, Meghna has worked
as an assistant director to her father, veteran
Gulzar, in *Hu Tu Tu* (1999), and to Saeed
Akhtar Mirza in *Naseem* (1995).

God knows tinsel town is brimming over
with self-confidence: Mira Nair's triumph at
Venice (Golden Lion) shows that Indian
cinema may finally be crossing over to global
mainstream. Beyond cinema theatres which
cater to connoisseurs of parallel and third
world cinema-or in the case of Indian cinema
to the Indian diaspora the world over and to
pockets in North Africa and the former
Soviet Union. And now *Lagaan*, pure
Bollywood, had the audience dancing in

the aisles overseas, and recently got the
audience award at the Locarno Film Festival–
it also made it to the top 20 in the UK.
Shah Rukh Khan's period film *Asoka* (another
mainstream Indian film) was screened at
Venice and will be commercially released in
Japan. The other reason for glee: Baz
Luhrmann's incredibly kitsch *Moulin Rouge*
(2001) was nothing if not pure Bollywood. With
melodrama at high tide and one song close
upon the heels of another, Nicole Kidman and
Ewan McGregor looked like a leading pair in
a Hindi film, only white. Even Luhrmann
acknowledged the inspiration: he spent some
time in India before he made the film and has
often said that he learned a great deal from
popular Hindi cinema. Another homage to
Bollywood in the aisles: Andrew Lloyd Webber
(Cats, Phantom of the Opera) is presently
working on a musical about Bollywood,
Bombay Dreams which will have music by
A.R. Rahman. In other words: they are
playing our song.

INDEX

Editorial advisors

DEREK MALCOLM

Derek Malcolm has been the film critic for the *Guardian*, London for more than three decades and is internationally acclaimed for his writings on world cinema. He extensively covered the rise of new cinema in India in the 1970s and 1980s and has served on several international film festival juries. Derek Malcolm has played a significant role in promoting Indian cinema in the UK and was the director of the London International Film Festival in the early 1980s. He is also the president of the International Film Critics' Association (FIPRESCI). His recent book, *Personal Best: A Century of Films* (Tauris Parke Paperbacks, London), includes an assessment of Bollywood films.

P. K. NAIR

P. K. Nair headed the National Film Archive of India, Pune for nearly three decades and virtually built it up from scratch to an institution of interna-tional reckoning. He played a leading role in developing film studies in the country and in inspiring the students of the Film & Television Institute of India (FTII), Pune. The FTII is India's premier institution, producing a new breed of filmmakers with a radical approach to cinema. P. K. Nair is a leading authority on Indian cinema and has guided many research workers in India and abroad. A dedicated film historian and film scholar, he has undertaken an in-depth study of Indian silent cinema and written extensively on various aspects of the evolution of cinema in India.

Editor

LALIT MOHAN JOSHI

An authority on Indian cinema, Lalit Mohan Joshi has been extensively writing and commenting on the subject for more than two decades. A founder-member of South Asian Cinema Foundation (SACF), London, he is the Editor *of South Asian Cinema*, the UK's first quarterly journal on the subject. Lalit Mohan Joshi joined BBC World Service, London as a producer in the Hindi Service in 1988; in 1991 he conceived and presented an acclaimed nineteen-part radio feature series on the history of Indian cinema. He joined BBC Television (Pebble Mill) in 1993, and was one of the main producers for the first TV quiz programme on Hindi cinema in Britain: 'Bollywood or Bust' (BBC2, 1994-95).

As a curator and Indian cinema programmer at the Birmingham International Film and TV Festival (1994-99), he raised the profile of South Asian Cinema in the UK. Besides writing for the *Guardian* (London), *India Today* and *Screen* (Mumbai), he is a leading consultant on South Asian cinema for the BBC, ITV, C4 and for mainstream radio in the UK.

Authors

GULZAR

Gulzar is a legendary figure of Indian cinema. His rather reluctant entry into Bollywood, through a song for Bimal Roy's *Bandini* in the late 1950s, brought him instant fame. After graduating into filmmaking with Bimal Roy, Gulzar eventually rose to become a celebrity lyricist, screenwriter and filmmaker. *Aandhi, Mausam, Ijaazat* and *Machis* are his landmark films. Gulzar believes that *Aandhi* was the first mainstream film with a proper political comment. Most of his films explore socially relevant themes. As an independent screenwriter, his *New Delhi Times* is a classic on account of its chilling realism.

Beyond filmmaking Gulzar is an acclaimed Urdu poet. What makes him conspicuous as a poet is his imagery, which is rooted in India's rural and folk traditions as well as the philosophical depth of Indian (eastern) thought. Gulzar is also a film academic and has written extensively on the history of lyrics and music in India's popular Hindi cinema.

SHYAM BENEGAL

Shyam Benegal is a pioneer of 'new cinema' in India. His debut film *Ankur* was a real breakthrough that defied all the ground rules of popular Hindi cinema. Benegal's first three films - *Ankur, Nishant* and *Manthan* form a thematic trilogy. It was their popular acclaim that made him a prominent figure of Hindi cinema in the 1970s and 1980s. Later, via films like *Bhumika* and *Junoon*, Benegal created a middle ground between the realms of art and commercial cinema. His films struck a chord among both discerning and ordinary filmgoers.

Shyam Benegal is one of the most highly celebrated Indian filmmakers in the west, after Satyajit Ray. He has introduced more acting talent into the world of Indian films than any other filmmaker. These include: Shabana Azmi, Smita Patil, Naseeruddin Shah, Om Puri, Rajit Kapur and very recently Rahul Maharya in *Zubeidaa*.

PRATIK JOSHI

Pratik Joshi is a documentary filmmaker and film critic based in New Delhi. His video film *Living With Clams* won an award from the Northwest Broadcast News Association, USA in 1998. After gaining an MA in History from St Stephen's College, Delhi, he has worked as a freelance journalist since the late 1980s, writing about popular culture for the major Indian national dailies including the *Hindustan Times* and the *Pioneer*. He earned his second Master's degree in Broadcast Journalism from the University of Minnesota, and has worked as a print journalist and as a news producer for a satellite news channel based in Minneapolis.

Recently Pratik Joshi has been one of the editors for the yearly film publications of the Directorate of Film Festivals, New Delhi. He is also a script consultant and teaches history and journalism at Delhi University.

MAITHILI RAO

An English lecturer turned film critic, Maithili Rao has been reviewing films and writing on Indian cinema for the last twenty years. She is a regular contributor to the daily *Hindu* and *Gentleman*. Her articles have appeared in the *Deccan Herald, Illustrated Weekly of India, Screen, Bombay* and *Premier*, and she has also contributed chapters to *Frames of Mind* edited by Aruna Vasudev, and *Rasa* edited by Chidananda Das Gupta.

Maithili Rao has served on international juries - FIPRESCI at Sochi, International Children's Film Festival (Hyderabad), and the Documentary Film Festival, Bombay. She is also a member of the Children's Film Society script committee. Editor of the brochure of the Mumbai International Film Festival for the past three years, she also subtitles Hindi, Telugu and Kannada feature films into English for film festivals and the international market - an essential tool in projecting Indian cinema all over the world.

DEEPA GAHLOT

Deepa Gahlot is a journalist and film critic of over eighteen years' standing. She has written extensively on film, theatre, culture, women's issues, travel and a variety of subjects. Her writings have appeared in reputed journals, anthologies and cinema publications. She has worked on documentaries, TV programmes, video films, radio, and the Internet and also written a children's film. She won the National Award for Best Film Criticism in 1998.

Deepa Gahlot has been on selection committees and juries for film festivals and awards. She is currently on the script selection committee of the Children's Film Society of India. She has also lectures on women and the media at seminars and women's studies courses. Her current projects include a monograph on filmmaker Hrishikesh Mukherjee, a documentary and NFDC's journal *Cinema* in India.

MADHU JAIN

Madhu Jain is a well-known journalist who has been writing for almost thirty years on a wide range of subjects from politics, social trends and the study of Indian society to the arts and popular culture. Cinema is an abiding interest. During her fourteen-year stint with India's leading news magazine *India Today*, where she was a senior editor, she wrote extensively on different aspects of Indian cinema. She has covered international and regional film festivals for many years and her analysis and appraisal of popular as well as new Indian cinema has been significant.

Educated in India, USA, and Paris (Sorbonne), Madhu Jain has previously worked for the *Statesman*, and was for many years the New Delhi correspondent of the French daily *La Croix*. At present, she is working on two books on Indian cinema.

DOLLY THAKORE

Dolly Thakore is a well-known art and film critic who has written extensively on theatre and films in various newspapers and magazines. She began her career with the BBC World Service where she worked between 1965 and 1969. Dolly was an editorial assistant for London Calling and worked as a research assitant on 24-Hours. She has also worked for Doordarshan and All India Radio. She has wide experience in communications and public affairs and has been a consultant for firms like B4U, Proctor & Gamble and Genesis PR.

Dolly Thakore has served on the National Film Jury in India. She has moderated international trade fairs and seminars, compèred numerous international festivals and arranged art auctions for charities. For over twenty years she has been a casting director for foreign films including *Gandhi, Kim, Jinnah, Such a Long Journey, Indiana Jones* and *Trying to Grow*. She recently edited the brochure for the Mumbai International Documentary Film Festival. She is also a recognized actress in English theatre in India.

IMAGE SOURCES

Special thanks to:

Gulzar

Shyam Benegal

K.S. Sashidharan, NFAI

A. Durga Prasad
Aamir Khan Productions
Anil Saari Arora
B.R. Chopra
B4U
Consulate General of Switzerland, Mumbai
Fifth Dimension
Gautam Rajadhyaksha
Indrajeet Aurangabadrarj
Kamat Fotoflash
Nabeel Abbas
National Film Archive of India, Pune
Pramod K. Gupta
Rahul Nanda
Rajiv Rai, Trumtri Films
Ronee Naterwalla
Sascha Sippy
Sholay Media & Entertainment Ltd
Sony Entertainment Television
South Asian Cinema Foundation
Subash Ghai
Wadia Movietone Archives/Riyad
Vinci Wadia
Yashraj Films

Second Editon 2002
First published 2001
2001 Dakini Books Ltd

Dakini Books Ltd
211-212 Piccadilly
London W1J 9HG
T 020 7830 9692
F 020 7830 9693
www.dakinibooks.com

Publisher **Lucky Dissanayake**
Associate Publisher **Dolly Thakore**

Editorial Advisors **Derek Malcolm**, **PK Nair**
Editor **Lalit Mohan Joshi**
Sub-Editor **Pamela Johnston**
Photo Editor **Mani Suri**
Design **SMITH**
Printed in Italy

A CIP catalogue record for this book is available from the British Library

Library of Congress Cataloguing in Publication Data available.

ISBN 095370 32-2-3

With gratitude to the kind & generous support of